JOHN

Poems selected by PAUL MULDOON

John Donne (1572–1631) forfeited his Parliamentary seat and was briefly imprisoned when his secret marriage to Ann More was uncovered in 1601. He spent the subsequent decade in poverty, trying to rehabilitate his reputation. He entered the Church in 1615, and became Dean of St Paul's. His first volume of poetry was published posthumously in 1633.

Paul Muldoon was born in County Armagh in 1951. He is the author of eleven books of poetry, including *Moy Sand and Gravel* (2002), for which he received the Pulitzer Prize for Poetry, *Horse Latitudes* (2006) and *Maggot* (2010). Since 1987 he has lived in the United States, where he is the Howard G. B. Clark Professor in the Humanities at Princeton University. An Honorary Fellow of Hertford College, Oxford, and a Fellow of the Royal Society of Literature, Paul Muldoon was given an American Academy of Arts and Letters award in 1996.

IN THE POET-TO-POET SERIES

W. H. AUDEN – John Fuller
WILLIAM BARNES – Andrew Motion
JOHN BERRYMAN – Michael Hofmann
JOHN BETJEMAN – Hugo Williams
WILLIAM BLAKE – James Fenton
ROBERT BROWNING – Douglas Dunn
ROBERT BURNS – Don Paterson
LORD BYRON – Paul Muldoon
THOMAS CAMPION – Charles Simic
GEOFFREY CHAUCER – Bernard O'Donoghue
JOHN CLARE – Paul Farley
SAMUEL TAYLOR COLERIDGE – James Fenton
HART CRANE – Maurice Riordan
EMILY DICKINSON – Ted Hughes
JOHN DONNE – Paul Muldoon
KEITH DOUGLAS – Ted Hughes
JOHN DRYDEN – Charles Tomlinson
ALLEN GINSBERG – Mark Ford
THOM GUNN – August Kleinzahler
THOMAS HARDY – Tom Paulin
GEORGE HERBERT – Jo Shapcott
ROBERT HERRICK – Stephen Romer
GERARD MANLEY HOPKINS – John Stammers
A. E. HOUSMAN – Alan Hollinghurst
TED HUGHES – Simon Armitage
JOHN KEATS – Andrew Motion
D. H. LAWRENCE – Tom Paulin
ROBERT LOWELL – Michael Hofmann
LOUIS MACNEICE – Michael Longley
ANDREW MARVELL – Sean O'Brien
WILFRED OWEN – Jon Stallworthy
SYLVIA PLATH – Ted Hughes
EZRA POUND – Thom Gunn
SIR WALTER RALEGH – Ruth Padel
CHRISTINA ROSSETTI – Emma Jones
PERCY BYSSHE SHELLEY – Fiona Sampson
JOHN SKELTON – Anthony Thwaite
WALLACE STEVENS – John Burnside
JONATHAN SWIFT – Derek Mahon
ALFRED, LORD TENNYSON – Mick Imlah
DYLAN THOMAS – Derek Mahon
EDWARD THOMAS – Matthew Hollis
WILLIAM WORDSWORTH – Seamus Heaney
THOMAS WYATT – Alice Oswald
W. B. YEATS – Seamus Heaney

JOHN DONNE

Poems selected by PAUL MULDOON

faber and faber

First published in 2012
by Faber and Faber Ltd
Bloomsbury House, 74–77 Great Russell Street
London WC1B 3DA

Typeset by CB editions, London
Printed in England by CPI Group (UK) Ltd, Croydon CR0 4YY

All rights reserved
Selection and Introduction © Paul Muldoon, 2012

The right of Paul Muldoon to be identified as editor
of this work has been asserted in accordance with Section 77
of the Copyright, Designs and Patents Act 1988

This book is sold subject to the condition that it shall not,
by way of trade or otherwise, be lent, resold, hired out or
otherwise circulated without the publisher's prior consent
in any form of binding or cover other than that in which
it is published and without a similar condition including
this condition being imposed on the subsequent purchaser

A CIP record for this book
is available from the British Library

ISBN 978–0–571–23089–1

FSC
www.fsc.org
MIX
Paper from
responsible sources
FSC® C101712

TOWER HAMLETS LIBRARIES	
91000001465095	
Bertrams	16/07/2012
821.3	£5.99
THISCH	TH12001055

10 9 8 7 6 5 4 3 2 1

Contents

Introduction *All Done: The Completeness of the Dean* ix

Aire and Angels 3
ELEGIE II The Anagram 4
The Anniversarie 6
The Apparition 7
ELEGIE IX The Autumnall 8
The Baite 10
The Blossome 11
ELEGIE XI The Bracelet 13
Breake of Day 17
The Broken Heart 18
A Burnt Ship 19
The Canonization 20
ELEGIE III Change 22
Communitie 24
ELEGIE VIII The Comparison 25
The Computation 27
Confined Love 28
The Curse 29
The Dampe 30
The Dissolution 31
ELEGIE X The Dreame 32
The Extasie 33
The Expiration 36
Farewell to Love 37
A Feaver 39
The Flea 40
The Funerall 41
Song ('Goe, and catche a falling starre') 42
Goodfriday, 1613. Made as I was riding Westward that day 43
The Good-Morrow 45

ELEGIE V His Picture 46

Holy Sonnets I–XII 47

The Indifferent 53

ELEGIE I Jealosie 54

A Lecture upon the Shadow 55

The Legacie 56

Lovers Infinitenesse 57

Loves Alchymie 58

Loves Deitie 59

Loves Diet 60

Loves Exchange 61

Loves Growth 63

ELEGIE XVIII Loves Progress 64

Loves Usury 67

ELEGIE XX Loves Warre 68

The Message 70

ELEGIE VII 'Natures lay Ideot, I taught thee to love' 71

Negative Love 72

A Nocturnall upon S. Lucies Day, Being the shortest day 73

ELEGIE VI 'Oh let mee not serve so, as those men serve' 75

ELEGIE XVI On his Mistris 77

The Paradox 79

ELEGIE IV The Perfume 80

The Primrose 83

Of the Progresse of the Soule. The Second Anniversarie 84

The Prohibition 99

The Relique 100

DIVINE POEM XVIII 'Show me deare Christ, thy spouse,
  so bright and clear' 101

The Sunne Rising 102

Song ('Sweetest love, I do not goe') 103

To a Jeat Ring sent to me 105

To his Mistris, Going to bed 106

The Triple Foole 108

Twicknam Garden 109

The Undertaking 110
A Valediction: forbidding mourning 111
A Valediction: of my name, in the window 113
A Valediction: of the booke 116
A Valediction: of weeping 118
The Will 119
Witchcraft by a picture 121
Womans Constancy 122

Introduction *All Done: The Completeness of the Dean*

I

John Donne is, for many of us, the greatest English poet. He's not always been seen as such, of course, not even by normally reliable taste-makers such as S. T. Coleridge:

> With Donne, whose muse on dromedary trots,
> Wreathe iron pokers into true-love knots;
> Rhyme's sturdy cripple, fancy's maze and clue,
> Wit's forge and fire-blast, meaning's press and screw.

Coleridge's representation of the poet as blowhard, buffoon and blunderer had already had some currency in his lifetime, when Ben Jonson reported to Drummond of Hawthornden that while Donne was 'the first poet in the world in some things' there was a problem with his 'not keeping of accent', for which 'he deserved hanging'.

Ben Jonson's view of the unreliably lumbering and lurching aspect of Donne's metrics was taken up by his near namesake, Doctor Samuel Johnson, who generalised about the lynch-worthiness of an entire group of poets he described as 'metaphysical', whom he describes as 'a race of writers' (perhaps influencing Coleridge's image of the racing camel) who appeared 'about the beginning of the seventeenth century':

> The metaphysical poets were men of learning, and to show their learning was their whole endeavour; but, unluckily resolving to show it in rhyme, instead of writing poetry they only wrote verses and very often such verses as stood the trial of the finger better than the ear; for the modulation was so imperfect, that they were only found to be verses by counting the syllables.

In addition to writing verses that 'stood the trial of the finger better than the ear', Donne was the target of finger pointing by

Johnson when it came to the kind of wit Johnson diagnosed as metaphysical:

> But wit, abstracted from its effects upon the hearer, may be more rigorously and philosophically considered as a kind of *Discordia concors*; a combination of dissimilar images, or discovery of occult resemblances in things apparently unlike. Of wit, thus defined, they have more than enough. The most heterogeneous ideas are yoked by violence together; nature and art are ransacked for illustrations, comparisons, and allusions; their learning instructs, and their subtlety surprises; but the reader commonly thinks his improvement dearly bought, and, though he sometimes admires, is seldom pleased.

This theme is picked up by Dryden, who followed Johnson by insisting of Donne:

> He affects the metaphysics, not only in his satires, but in his amorous verses, where nature only should reign; and perplexes the minds of the fair sex with nice speculations of philosophy, when he should engage their hearts, and entertain them with the softnesses of love.

A poem which is quite typical of what Dryden calls Donne's 'amorous verses' is 'The Good-Morrow' (page 45). I propose to spend some time in ransacking it (I borrow the term from Doctor Johnson, of course) and, by the time I've looted it for its infinite riches, trust I'll have persuaded myself once more that it's a poem of which, in one of those 'nice speculations of philosophy', we may make of 'one little roome, an every where'. It's certainly a poem that's remarkably capacious in its ability to take in the wide range of Donne's aberrations and abrogations and to underscore the complex continuity of a poet more generally thought of as out-and-out rake or out-and-out rector.

The title of the poem is typically direct and directorial. We find ourselves in a well-used 'little room' in which the tradition of the morning song has flourished at least as far back as Catullus:

Come and let us live my Deare,
Let us love and never feare,
What the sowrest Fathers say:
Brightest *Sol* that dyes to day
Lives again as blithe to morrow,
But if we darke sons of sorrow
Set; o then, how long a Night
Shuts the Eyes of our short light!
Then let amorous kisses dwell
On our lips, begin and tell
A Thousand, and a Hundred, score
An Hundred, and a Thousand more,
Till another Thousand smother
That, and that wipe of another.
Thus at last when we have numbred
Many a Thousand, many a Hundred;
We'll confound the reckoning quite,
And lose our selves in wild delight;
While our joyes so multiply,
As shall mocke the envious eye.

I've quoted at length from this version of Catullus 5 by
Richard Crashaw largely to point out that, given the antiquity
of '*nobis cum semel occidit brevis lux,/ nox est perpetua una dor-
mienda*', Donne should have been recognised by Ben Jonson
as being anything but 'first' in the sense of new, while Samuel
Johnson could easily have traced the form of wit he recognised
as *Discordia concors* to Catullus's smart-ass musings from the
first century BC. The tradition of the *alba* or 'dawn song' had
developed from the Occitan tradition through the German
minnesingers and the French trouvères' *aube* and made its way
into English literature with Chaucer's *Troilus and Criseyde*:

O cruel day, accusor of the joie
That nyght and love han stole and faste iwryen,
Acorsed be thi coming into Troye,
For every bore hath oon of thi bryghte yen!

The time-honoured complaint against the interruption by day of the joys of the night is the burden of several aubades by Donne, notably 'The Sunne Rising:'

Busie old foole, unruly Sunne,
Why dost thou thus,
Through windowes, and through curtaines call on us?

The wonderfully in-your-face tone of the speaker's calling out to, and calling out, the sun is a hallmark of Donne's poetry. One of the 'things' in which Donne is surely 'the first poet in the world' is in his handling of first lines. The first line of 'The Good-Morrow', with its combination of launching an offensive (the in-your-face tone I mentioned a moment ago) and off-handedness, is no exception:

I wonder by my troth, what thou, and I
Did, till we lov'd?

The phrase 'by my troth' establishes the conspiratorial relation-ship between the speaker of the poem and his beloved, but it also manages to draw in the reader and somehow implicate her. It's as if a vow has been taken, an oath sworn. The phrase is familiar to us from a number of Shakespeare's plays, including *Hamlet* and Act 3, Scene 4 of *Much Ado About Nothing*:

MARGARET: Troth, I think your other *rebato* were better.
HERO: No, pray thee, good Meg, I'll wear this.
MARGARET: By my troth, is not so good; and I warrant your cousin will say so.
HERO: My cousin's a fool, and thou art another. I'll wear none but this.
MARGARET: I like the new *tire* within excellently, if the hair were a thought browner; and your gown's a most rare fashion, i' faith. I saw the Duchess of Milan's gown that they praise so.
HERO: O, that exceeds, they say.
MARGARET: By my troth, 's but a night gown in respect of

yours; cloth o' gold, and cuts, and laced with silver, set with
pearls, down sleeves, side sleeves, and skirts, round under-
borne with a bluish tinsel: but for a fine, quaint, graceful
and excellent fashion, yours is worth ten on 't.

HERO: God give me joy to wear it! For my heart is exceed-
ing heavy.

MARGARET: 'Twill be heavier soon by the weight of a man.

This last line confirms the blue undertow of the scene
that would already have elicited snorts and sniggers from
an Elizabethan audience. As Eric Partridge reminds us, in
Shakespeare's Bawdy, the word 'gown', for example, is rendered
as *coun* by Princess Katherine in that infamous scene in *Henry
IV* as an 'approximation' to the French *con* (pudend). That
this exchange might be a comparison of the relative merits of
pudenda is confirmed by the occurrence of the word 'quaint', a
term we recognise from its appearance in that most famous of
chat-up poems, Andrew Marvell's 'To His Coy Mistress', which
takes advantage of the same naughty pun:

Thy beauty shall no more be found,
Nor, in thy marble vault, shall sound
My echoing song: then worms shall try
That long preserv'd virginity,
And your *quaint* honor turn to dust,
And into ashes all my lust.

The proximity of 'virginity' and the 'quaint' is similarly found
in lines 2 and 3 of 'The Good-Morrow':

were we not wean'd till then?
But suck'd on *countrey* pleasures, childishly?

This is the same naughty pun Hamlet uses to Ophelia when
he asks her 'Or did you think I meant country matters?' and
it sends me back to the phrase that straddles the end of line 1
and the beginning of line 2 of 'The Good-Morrow', the rather
innocuous 'I/ Did.' To 'do', as the redoubtable Eric Partridge

reminds us, means 'to copulate with'. Partridge gives examples from *Titus Andronicus* ('I have done thy mother') and *Measure for Measure* ('What has he done? – A woman'). Now, this is a pun that must have had a particular relevance for someone whose name is Donne. Indeed, it's a pun Donne often used of himself and, memorably, of his relationship with Ann More, whom he secretly married in 1601:

John Donne.
Ann Donne.
Undone.

II

Even before his marriage to Ann More, though, John Donne had led a vigorous, varied and vicissitude-ridden life. Born in London in 1572, he was brought up by his mother, his father, also known as John Donne, having died when Donne was four. The impact of a father's death on a young child is a major one, one compounded by other sadnesses. It's generally thought that the name Donne is Welsh, though some of us believe his family to be very closely linked to the Irish sept of the O'Doinn or O'Duinn. The Irish word *donn*, like its Welsh cognate *dwyn*, means 'dark' or 'brown-haired' and it appears widely as Dunn or Dunne, so much so that it is now the 27th most common surname in Ireland. In the mid-sixteenth century the Dunnes of Leinster, the province separated from Wales by a mere 40 miles of sea, were notorious for being particularly hostile to the English establishment. Their Welsh cousins were, paradoxically, part of that very establishment. Donne's father was a prosperous merchant who was highly positioned in the Ironmongers Company. The hinterland of ironmongery may lie behind Coleridge's odd image of Donne's capacity to 'wreathe *iron* pokers into true love's knots'. As for Donne's mother, Elizabeth Heywood, I'll let Izaak Walton take up the story:

By his mother he was descended of the family of the famous and learned Sir Thomas More, sometime Lord Chancellor of England: as also, from that worthy and laborious Judge Rastall, who left Posterity the vast statutes of the law of this nation most exactly abridged.

In any case, John Donne entered Hart Hall (now Hertford College), Oxford, in 1584, at the age of eleven. Between 1587 and 1590 Donne was at Cambridge University. In neither institution did he receive a degree, however, since he refused to take the Oath of Supremacy that recognised the English monarch as head of the church. The critical fact here is that Donne had been raised as a Catholic and was, indeed, tutored by two Jesuits, Ellis and Jasper Heywood, who just happened to be his uncles. It's worth remembering that the Jesuits had been established in 1534 by Ignatius Loyola, a mere fifty years before Donne entered Hart Hall. The Society of Jesus was also known as the 'Company' of Jesus, a designation that underlined Ignatius Loyola's ambition that the Jesuits be a kind of spiritual militia at the service of the Pope who, in 1540, sanctioned the idea that he should be served by this private army. As René Fülöp-Miller puts it, in his study of *The Power and Secret of the Jesuits*:

For, within a short time after the foundation of the order, the Jesuits were acting as spiritual directors at the courts of Europe, as preachers in the most remote primeval forests, as political conspirators, disguised and in constant danger of death; thus they had a thousand opportunities to employ their talents, their cleverness, their knowledge of the world, and even their cunning.

Something of that 'cunning' may be seen to have moulded the young Donne. Indeed, the trope of a personality being 'moulded' is a key one in Jesuitical education, as members of the order were required to give themselves over to, or put themselves in the hands of, their General 'as a lump of wax is kneaded'. The image often used of Jesuitical obedience is that the soldier be 'corpse-like', the ideal state for following orders. As René Fülöp-Miller reminds us, the basic tenet of the Jesuits is that 'to whom the end is permitted, to him also are permitted the means ordered to the end'. That the ends might justify the means allows for the quality that we most associate with the word Jesuitical – 'having the character ascribed to the Jesuits; deceitful, dissembling; practicing equivocation, prevarication, or mental reservation of truth' (*OED*). Such 'mental reservation of truth' might include casuistry of the calibre condoned by Alphonsus de Liguori (1696–1787) in his *Tractatus de Secundo Decalogi Praecepto*:

> It is permissible to swear to anything which is false by adding in an undertone a true condition, if that low utterance can in any way be perceived by the other party, though its sense is not understood.

I want to propose that John Donne was instilled with a facility to talk out of both sides of his mouth, a facility for which the Jesuits were expelled from England in 1584 – the year in which, again, Donne arrived in Hart Hall. The date is somewhat random, I must say, since the Jesuits had already been expelled from England in 1579 and 1581, just as they would be expelled yet again in 1586, 1602 and 1604. As it happens, his uncle Jasper, whose own poems had been included in the 1576 anthology *A Paradise of Dainty Devices*, had been made superior of the Jesuit mission to England in 1581 and, after being imprisoned in the Tower of London from December 1583 to January 1585, was sent into exile. What Donne knew intimately, then, was the harsh reality of imprisonment for one's religious beliefs. The story of the seven sleepers of Ephesus, to which he alludes in line 4 of 'The Good-Morrow', was one that had more than faint resonances with his own family history. Indeed, the story of the seven Christian men who hid in a cave somewhere near Ephesus in about 250 AD to escape the persecution of Christians by the emperor Decius and fell asleep, only to be sealed within their prison for 150–200 years and discovered during the reign of

Theodosius II (408–450), was one that Donne almost certainly knew from a dramatic piece published in 1544 and entitled *The playe called the foure PP . . . A palmer. A pardoner. A potycary. A peddler.* This play, in which the Pardoner is offering a relic in the form of 'a slipper/ Of one of the Seven Sleepers', happens to have been written by John Heywood, Donne's maternal grandfather and the father of his tutors, Ellis and Jasper. Donne draws on the imagery of Roman Catholic gobbledygook and geegaws in a number of his poems, most memorably in 'The Relique' itself:

> When my grave is broke up againe
> Some second ghest to entertaine,
> (For graves have learn'd that woman-head
> To be to more then one a Bed)
>   And he that digs it, spies
> A bracelet of bright haire about the bone,
>   Will he not let'us alone,
> And thinke that there a loving couple lies,
> Who thought that this device might be some way
> To make their soules, at the last busie day,
> Meet at this grave, and make a little stay?

The continuing impact of the Heywoods on Donne's imagination is clear from at least two usages in 'The Relique'. I'm thinking of the word 'device', which sends me right back to *A Paradise of Dainty Devices*, the title of the anthology in which Jasper Heywood has appeared, as well as the word 'spies' and its boatload of associations with the world of spectre and subterfuge in which the Heywoods so fearfully moved. While it's likely, then, that Donne knew the story of the seven sleepers from his Jesuit uncles' knees, he would also become aware of the perils of religious nonconformity from his even more immediate family. In 1593, his younger brother, Henry, would be accused of harbouring a Catholic priest, imprisoned in Newgate and threatened with torture. At the time of Henry's death, at the age of nineteen, from the bubonic plague he contracted in Newgate, John Donne had enrolled as a law student, first at Thavies Inn and then Lincoln's Inn. It's from this period that we have two tantalising glimpses of the poet as young man about town. From Izaak Walton we have the snapshot of a diligent scholar who would work during the early to mid-morning before going on to 'survey and consider the Body of Divinity, as it was then controverted betwixt the Reformed and the Roman Church', since, despite his brother's fate, he was then 'unresolv'd what religion to adhere to'. The other snapshot of Donne is by Sir Richard Baker and has him 'not dissolute, but very neat'. It's Baker who also gives us the thumbnail sketch of Donne as being 'a great visitor of Ladies, a great frequenter of Playes, a great writer of conceited Verses'. This description is of a piece with George Best's description of his wayward lifestyle ('I spent most of my money on women and drink – the rest I just frittered away') and has resulted in the rather geometrically crude version of Donne's story being, as Walton proposed, that 'the English Church had gain'd a second St Augustine'. The image presented in 'The Good-Morrow' is of lovers who are adept and adaptable, who have been weaned from an infantile or childish sucking on 'countrey pleasures' to being in an adult condition in which 'all pleasures fancies be'. The word 'fancies' is one that is worth pausing over, particularly since, as a contraction of fantasy, it was being used by Richard Hooker in his *Laws of Ecclesiastical Polity* (the first four books of which were published in 1593, the year of Henry Donne's death, the fifth appearing in 1597), to describe the delusive imagination based on apparition rather than informed by reason:

The righteous may have their *phancies*; they may conceive worse of their own estate than reason giveth.

In that very year, 1597, one of the plays Donne may have frequented was *Henry IV, Part 1*, in which Shakespeare gives us one of the first usages of fancy (one to which Coleridge alludes in '*fancy*'s maze and clue') as 'a composition in an impromptu style':

> He was the very genius of famine; yet lecherous as a monkey, and the whores call'd him mandrake: he came ever in the rearward of the fashion; he sang those tunes to the over scutched housewives that he heard the carmen whistle, and aware – they were his *fancies*, or his good-nights.

This description of Shallow (of which and whom Eric Partridge ventures with uncustomary timidity, 'perhaps he was insatiable and monstrously perverted in his sexual practices') is spoken by none other than Falstaff. In 1597, we may recall, that character was still known as Oldcastle. Shakespeare felt it politic to delete any reference to Sir John Oldcastle, the Protestant martyr on whom he's based. Oldcastle was a Lollard, who had escaped imprisonment in the Tower of London only to be hanged and burned over a slow fire in St Giles Field in 1417, an image that might have reminded Donne of the death in 1594 of William Harrington, the priest harboured by Henry Donne, who was hanged and drawn at Tyburn. Sir John Oldcastle had at least one descendant, William Brooke, who just happened to be Lord Chamberlain between 1596 and 1597, and just happened to give Shakespeare and his acting troupe, the Lord Chamberlain's Men, a hard time over the besmirching of his ancestor's name. Yet again, Shakespeare's decision was based on political expediency in a time of religious uncertainty, one in which meaning could literally be pressed and screwed from a suspect. I myself suspect that Donne's use of the word 'fancies' is informed by these lines from *Henry IV*, particularly when the contiguous 'good-nights' in Shakespeare have now given way to Donne's 'Good-*Morrow*'. The 'phancies' of the 'judicious' Richard Hooker are also part of the weft of this extraordinary poem, since Hooker is a kind of Protestant Jesuit, his much vaunted *via media* another way of describing the ability to talk through both sides of his mouth, insisting that there's a middle ground between the extremes of Catholic reliance on tradition and Protestant reliance on

Scripture which may be occupied by the element of human Reason. We see the essence of such sophistry in the outrageous second stanza of 'The Flea':

> Oh stay, three lives in one flea spare,
> Where wee almost, yea more then maryed are,
> This flea is you and I, and this
> Our mariage bed, and mariage temple is;
> Though parents grudge, and you, w'are met,
> And cloysterd in these living walls of Jet.
>   Though use make you apt to kill mee,
>   Let not to that, selfe murder added bee,
>   And sacrilege, three sinnes in killing three.

Though Hooker had been elected a Fellow of Corpus Christ College in 1577, he left Oxford in 1584, the year Donne arrived at Hart Hall, so Donne probably wasn't familiar with Hooker at Oxford. He may have known him in London, however, given Hooker's prominence as a preacher and scholar of scripture:

> Adam is in us as an original cause of our nature, and of that corruption of nature which causeth death, Christ as the cause original of restoration to life; the person of Adam is not in us, but his nature, and the corruption of his nature derived unto all men by propagation; Christ having Adam's nature as we have, but incorrupt, deriveth not nature but incorruption and that immediately from his own person into all that belong unto him. As therefore we are really partakers of the body of sin and death received from Adam, so except we be truly partakers of Christ, and as really possessed of his Spirit, all we speak of eternal life is but a dream.

I want to propose that it's no mere coincidence that that last line I quote from book five of *The Lawes of Ecclesiastical Polity* is picked up in lines 6 and 7 of 'The Good-Morrow':

> If ever any beauty I did see,
> Which I desir'd, and got, t'was *but a dreame* of thee.

Donne has taken Hooker's sacred argument about the sacrament of the Eucharist and given it a secular twist, so that this manifestation of the point at which time and eternity intersect as 'an outward and visible sign of an inward and invisible grace' is itself restored to new life. It's no accident that the iconography of the 'seaven sleepers' and the lovers in their 'one little roome' are connected to the Christ in his tomb, about to rise into a state of eternal life. God and mankind are connected in Hooker's mind in the person of the Sovereign, of course, the king of England. His assertion of the sovereign's supremacy included the Jesuitical idea that the safety of the realm demanded a militaristic unity and obedience from its subjects. Those who are disloyal, as Donne now found himself to be, and who 'strike at the State Ecclesiastical', according to Hooker, 'secretly wound the Civil State', By 1597, the year of publication of book five of *The Lawes of Ecclesiastical Polity*, John Donne's position in the Civil State looked fairly secure. That same year had seen him accompany the Earl of Essex and Sir Walter Raleigh against the Spanish in the Azores, just as the previous year had seen him in action in Cadiz. In 'The Calme', he gives a brilliantly observed account of life on a becalmed boat where 'as water did in storms, now pitch runs out/ As lead, when a fired church becomes one spout'. This is doubly effective, both as a description of tar melting on a becalmed sun-beaten ship, but also as an indicator that the author might be open to the idea of firing the naves of certain churches. Donne picks up on the imagery of religious persecution as the poem progresses:

And on the hatches as on altars lies
Each one, his own priest, and own sacrifice.
Who live, that miracle do multiply
Where walkers in hot ovens, do not die.

Donne here appeals to the imagery of *The Book of Daniel* and its milieu of the persecution of the Jews in Babylon and the attempt by Nebuchadnezzar to force them to worship false idols, the casting of Shadrach, Meshach and Abed-Nego into the fiery furnace from which they emerge unscathed and, of course, the casting of Daniel himself into the lions' den. That explains, I should say, what might otherwise seem like the odd choice of the word 'den' in the phrase 'seaven sleepers *den*'. You'll notice the double meaning of the pivotal word 'lies' in the phrase 'And on the hatches as on altars *lies*/ Each one his own priest', again with the suggestion that priests like William Harrington might indeed be guilty of telling falsehoods and it being not inappropriate that they suffer the consequences. Donne was himself a 'sea-discoverer' of sorts, going to what then seemed like the 'new worlds' of the Azores. As he wrote to his fellow voyager, and fellow student at Hart Hall, Sir Henry Wotton:

Life is a voyage, and in our life's ways
Countries, courts, towns are rocks, or remoraes;
They break or stop all ships, yet our state's such,
That though than pitch they stain worse, we must touch.
If in the furnace of the even line,
Or under the' adverse icy poles thou pine,
Thou know'st two temperate regions girded in,
Dwell there.

This classic description of the *via media* might well be Richard Hooker's motto. We recognise some of the same ideas in the last stanza of 'The Good-Morrow' with its 'where can we finde two better hemispheares/ Without sharpe North, without declining West?'

The opening of 'To Sir Henry Wotton' also shares some of the same vocabulary as the second stanza of 'The Good-Morrow':

Sir, more than kisses, letters mingle *souls*;
For, thus friends absent speak. This ease *controls*
The tediousness of my life but for these
I could ideate nothing, which could please,
But I should wither in one day and pass
To a bottle of hay, that am a lock of grass.

Something of the proverbial hangs over these lines, ranging from the Biblical 'All flesh is grass' and 'He that toucheth pitch shall be defiled therewith' to a wispish echo of 'When the sun shineth, make hay', which just happens to have first appeared in *The Proverbs of John Heywood*, John Donne's maternal grandfather, and a punster on the first component of his first name. This trait, as we know, is one admired by Donne, as we see yet again in the last lines of 'To Sir Henry Wotton':

> But, Sir, I advise not you, I rather doe
> Say o'er those lessons, which I learn'd of you:
> Whom, free from German schismes, and lightnesse
> Of France, and fair Italies faithlesnesse,
> Having from these suck'd all they had of worth,
> And brought home that faith, which you carried forth,
> I throughly love. But if my selfe, I'have wonne
> To know my rules, I have, and you have   DONNE.

III

Which brings us back to that formulation I quoted earlier having to do with the impact on Donne's life of Ann More. Ann More was the niece of Sir Thomas Egerton, the Lord Keeper of the Great Seal of England, to whom the recently returned 'sea-discoverer' Donne was appointed secretary in 1597. Her father, George More, was Lieutenant of the Tower of London. All the evidence suggested that Donne, having now renounced Catholicism, had made it big. Unfortunately, he decided to marry Ann More secretly in 1601. When this became known the following year he was imprisoned briefly in the Fleet and dismissed from his secretarial post. It wasn't until 1615, when he was ordained as an Anglican priest, that things began to look a little brighter for Donne. In 1621, Donne was installed as Dean of St Paul's, where he remained until his death in 1631. Ann had predeceased him in 1617, having borne their twelfth child, a stillbirth. Donne's 'Holy Sonnet xvii' is addressed to his dead wife:

Since she whom I loved hath paid her last debt
To nature, and to hers and my good, is dead,
And her soul early into heaven ravished,
Wholly in heavenly things my mind is set.

Even now, Donne can't quite resist the pun on 'wholly' and 'holy', partly because it extends his system of imagery that he alludes to in 'Holy Sonnet 5' with its assertion that 'I am a little world made cunningly'. Even now he can't resist a schoolboyish snigger on the female anatomy. Something of Donne's method of taking an idea and running with it is set down as follows:

> In all Metricall compositions the force of the whole piece is for the most part left to the shutting up; the whole frame of the Poem is a beating out of a piece of gold, but the last clause is as the impression of the stamp, and that is what makes it currant.

This 'piece of gold' is highly reminiscent of the Jesuits' 'lump of wax', and it's an image to which Donne returns in 'A Valediction: forbidding mourning':

Our two soules therefore, which are one,
    Though I must goe, endure not yet
A breach, but an expansion,
    Like gold to ayery thinnesse beate.

If they be two, they are two so
    As stiffe twin compasses are two,
Thy soule the fixt foot, makes no show
    To move, but doth, if the'other doe.

It was precisely such an image of comparing the relationship of lovers to the legs of a compass that had Doctor Johnson wonder if 'absurdity or ingenuity has the better claim'. Even T. S. Eliot, that stalwart champion of Donne, refers to his 'distended metaphors and similes', and it's likely he's thinking of the lengths to which Donne will go to follow down his conceit:

And though it in the center sit,
    Yet when the other far doth rome,
It leanes, and hearkens after it,
    And growes erect, as that comes home.

The slackness associated with death in, say, 'The Second Anniversarie (of the Progress of the Soul)', with its 'Think thee laid on thy death-bed, loose and *slack*/ And think that but unbinding of a pack' is carried over into the final stanza of 'The Good Morrow':

My face in thine eye, thine in mine appeares,
And true plain hearts doe in the faces rest,
Where can we finde two better hemispheares
Without sharpe North, without declining West?
What ever dyes, was not mixt equally;
If our two loves be one, or, thou and I
Love so alike, that none doe slacken, none can die.

The progress of the soul is also described in 'Goodfriday, 1613' in terms of key cardinal points:

Hence is't, that I am carryed towards the West
This day, when my Soules forme bends toward the East.
There I should see a Sunne, by rising set,
And by that setting endlesse day beget;
But that Christ on this Crosse, did rise and fall,
Sinne had eternally benighted all.

The play on the homophonic Sun and the *Son* of God suggests yet again the inability to distinguish the vocabulary of one of Donne's celestial poems, such as 'Goodfriday, 1613', from that of an essentially salty one such as 'The Good-Morrow'. The union of bodies, in which two were thought to make one, is indivisible from the union of souls. One is reminded, indeed, that the tradition of the *alba* itself included both the sacred and sexy, the religious and randy 'dawn-songs'. A 'divine poem' such as 'Batter my heart, three person'd God' ends memorably with the paradox drawn from a system of imagery we might ordinarily consider down and dirty:

> Take me to you, imprison me, for I
> Except you enthrall me, never shall be free,
> Nor ever chaste, except you ravish me.

Meanwhile, a poem as solemn as 'A Hymn to God the Father' is no less punishingly punning in its refrain than the Ann More squib:

> When thou hast done, thou hast not done,
> For I have more.

In its final verse and refrain, the poem manages to transcend what might look like mere trickiness, referring as it does to Donne, his wife, and the sun/Son of God, to achieve a real sense of the tragic:

> I have a sin of fear, that when I have spun
> My last thread, I shall perish on the shore;
> But swear by thy self, that at my death thy *Son*
> Shall shine as he shines now, and heretofore;
> And, having *done* that, Thou hast done,
> I fear no *More*.

God the Father would indeed 'have' the Dean of St Paul's in 1631, but only after preaching his final sermon, 'Death's Duel':

> Our very birth and entrance into this life is *exitus a morte*, an issue from death, for in our mother's womb we are dead so, as that we do not know we live, not so much as we do in our sleep, neither is there any grave so close, or so putrid a prison, as the womb would be unto us, if we stayed in it beyond our time, or died there before our time.

Donne's musings on the womb are reminiscent of his musings in the second stanza of 'The Flea':

> In the womb the dead child kills the mother that conceived it, and is a murderer, nay a parricide, even after it is dead.

Donne continues with his familiar Jesuitical jousting:

> But then this *exitus a morte* is but *introitus in mortem*, this issue, this deliverance from that death, the death of the womb, is an entrance, a delivering over to another death, the manifold deaths of this world. We have a winding sheet in our Mother's womb, which grows with us from our conception, and we come into the world, wound up in that winding sheet, for we come to seek a grave.

No wonder, then, that Donne should so happily pose in his shroud for an artist. He kept the drawing of himself by his bedside and turned to it constantly. Punning to the end, his last words were, 'Thy Kingdom come, Thy Will be done.'

PAUL MULDOON

JOHN DONNE

Aire and Angels

Twice or thrice had I loved thee,
Before I knew thy face or name,
So in a voice, so in a shapelesse flame,
Angells affect us oft, and worship'd bee;
    Still when, to where thou wert, I came,
Some lovely glorious nothing I did see.
    But since my soule, whose child love is,
Takes limmes of flesh, and else could nothing doe,
    More subtile then the parent is,
Love must not be, but take a body too,
    And therefore what thou wert, and who,
        I bid Love aske, and now
That it assume thy body, I allow,
And fixe it selfe in thy lip, eye, and brow.

Whilst thus to ballast love, I thought,
And so more steddily to have gone,
With wares which would sinke admiration,
I saw, I had loves pinnace overfraught,
    Ev'ry thy haire for love to worke upon
Is much too much, some fitter must be sought;
    For, nor in nothing, nor in things
Extreme, and scatt'ring bright, can love inhere;
    Then as an Angell, face, and wings
Of aire, not pure as it, yet pure doth weare,
    So thy love may be my loves spheare;
        Just such disparitie
As is twixt Aire and Angells puritie,
Twixt womens love, and mens will ever bee.

Marry, and love thy *Flavia,* for, shee
Hath all things, whereby others beautious bee,
For, though her eyes be small, her mouth is great,
Though they be Ivory, yet her teeth be jeat,
Though they be dimme, yet she is light enough,
And though her harsh haire fall, her skinne is rough;
What though her cheeks be yellow, her haire's red,
Give her thine, and she hath a maydenhead.
These things are beauties elements, where these
Meet in one, that one must, as perfect, please.
If red and white and each good quality
Be in thy wench, ne'r aske where it doth lye.
In buying things perfum'd, we aske; if there
Be muske and amber in it, but not where.
Though all her parts be not in th'usuall place,
She'hath yet an Anagram of a good face.
If we might put the letters but one way,
In the leane dearth of words, what could wee say?
When by the Gamut some Musitions make
A perfect song, others will undertake,
By the same Gamut chang'd, to equall it.
Things simply good, can never be unfit.
She's faire as any, if all be like her,
And if none bee, then she is singular.
All love is wonder; if wee justly doe
Account her wonderfull, why not lovely too?
Love built on beauty, soone as beauty, dies,
Chuse this face, chang'd by no deformities.
Women are all like Angels; the faire be
Like those which fell to worse; but such as shee,
Like to good Angels, nothing can impaire:
'Tis lesse griefe to be foule, then to'have beene faire.
For one nights revels, silke and gold we chuse,

But, in long journeyes, cloth, and leather use.
Beauty is barren oft; best husbands say,
There is best land, where there is foulest way.
Oh what a soveraigne Plaister will shee bee,
If thy past sinnes have taught thee jealousie!
Here needs no spies, nor eunuches; her commit
Safe to thy foes; yea, to a Marmosit.
When Belgiaes citties, the round countries drowne,
That durty foulenesse guards, and armes the towne:
So doth her face guard her; and so, for thee,
Which, forc'd by businesse, absent oft must bee,
Shee, whose face, like clouds, turnes the day to night,
Who, mightier then the sea, makes Moores seem white,
Who, though seaven yeares, she in the Stews had laid,
A Nunnery durst receive, and thinke a maid,
And though in childbeds labour she did lie,
Midwifes would sweare, 'twere but a tympanie,
Whom, if shee accuse her selfe, I credit lesse
Then witches, which impossibles confesse,
Whom Dildoes, Bedstaves, and her Velvet Glasse
Would be as loath to touch as Joseph was:
One like none, and lik'd of none, fittest were,
For, things in fashion every man will weare.

The Anniversarie

All Kings, and all their favorites,
    All glory of honors, beauties, wits,
The Sun it selfe, which makes times, as they passe,
Is elder by a yeare, now, then it was
When thou and I first one another saw:
All other things, to their destruction draw,
    Only our love hath no decay;
This, no to morrow hath, nor yesterday,
Running it never runs from us away,
But truly keepes his first, last, everlasting day.

Two graves must hide thine and my coarse,
    If one might, death were no divorce
Alas, as well as other Princes, wee,
(Who Prince enough in one another bee,)
Must leave at last in death, these eyes, and eares,
Oft fed with true oathes, and with sweet salt teares;
    But soules where nothing dwells but love
(All other thoughts being inmates) then shall prove
This, or a love increased there above,
When bodies to their graves, soules from their graves remove.

And then wee shall be throughly blest,
    But wee no more, then all the rest;
Here upon earth, we'are Kings, and none but wee
Can be such Kings, nor of such subjects bee;
Who is so safe as wee? where none can doe
Treason to us, except one of us two.
    True and false feares let us refraine,
Let us love nobly, and live, and adde againe
Yeares and yeares unto yeares, till we attaine
To write threescore: this is the second of our raigne.

The Apparition

When by thy scorne, O murdresse, I am dead,
And that thou thinkst thee free
From all solicitation from mee,
Then shall my ghost come to thy bed,
And thee, fain'd vestall, in worse armes shall see;
Then thy sicke taper will begin to winke,
And he, whose thou art then, being tyr'd before,
Will, if thou stirre, or pinch to wake him, thinke
    Thou call'st for more,
And in false sleepe will from thee shrinke,
And then poore Aspen wretch, neglected thou
Bath'd in a cold quicksilver sweat wilt lye
    A veryer ghost then I;
What I will say, I will not tell thee now,
Lest that preserve thee'; and since my love is spent,
I'had rather thou shouldst painfully repent,
Then by my threatnings rest still innocent.

ELEGIE IX The Autumnall

No *Spring*, nor *Summer* Beauty hath such grace,
    As I have seen in one *Autumnall* face.
Yong *Beauties* force our love, and that's a *Rape*,
    This doth but *counsaile,* yet you cannot scape.
If t'were a *shame* to love, here t'were no *shame*,
    Affection here takes *Reverences* name.
Were her first yeares the *Golden Age;* That's true,
    But now shee's *gold* oft tried, and ever new.
That was her torrid and inflaming time,
    This is her tolerable *Tropique clyme.*
Faire eyes, who askes more heate then comes from hence,
    He in a fever wishes pestilence.
Call not these wrinkles, *graves*; If *graves* they were,
    They were *Loves graves*; for else he is no where.
Yet lies not Love *dead* here, but here doth sit
    Vow'd to this trench, like an *Anachorit.*
And here, till hers, which must be his *death,* come,
    He doth not digge a *Grave,* but build a *Tombe.*
Here dwells he, though he sojourne ev'ry where,
    In *Progresse,* yet his standing house is here.
Here, where still *Evening* is; not *noone,* nor *night*;
    Where no *voluptuousnesse,* yet all *delight.*
In all her words, unto all hearers fit,
    You may at *Revels,* you at *Counsaile,* sit.
This is loves timber, youth his under-wood;
    There he, as wine in *June,* enrages blood,
Which then comes seasonabliest, when our tast
    And appetite to other things, is past.
Xerxes strange *Lydian* love, the *Platane* tree,
    Was lov'd for age, none being so large as shee,
Or else because, being yong, nature did blesse
    Her youth with ages glory, *Barrennesse.*

If we love things long sought, *Age* is a thing
    Which we are fifty yeares in compassing.
If transitory things, which soone decay,
    Age must be lovelyest at the latest day.
But name not *Winter-faces,* whose skin's slacke;
    Lanke, as an unthrifts purse; but a soules sacke;
Whose *Eyes* seeke light within, for all here's shade;
    Whose *mouthes* are holes, ratherworne out, then made;
Whose every tooth to a severall place is gone,
    To vexe their soules at *Resurrection;*
Name not these living *Deaths-heads* unto mee,
    For these, not *Ancient,* but *Antique* be.
I hate extreames; yet I had rather stay
    With *Tombs,* then *Cradles,* to weare out a day.
Since such loves naturall lation is, may still
    My love descend, and journey downe the hill,
Not panting after growing beauties, so,
    I shall ebbe out with them, who home-ward goe.

The Baite

Come live with mee, and bee my love,
And we will some new pleasures prove
Of golden sands, and christall brookes,
With silken lines, and silver hookes.

There will the river whispering runne
Warm'd by thy eyes, more then the Sunne.
And there the'inamor'd fish will stay,
Begging themselves they may betray.

When thou wilt swimme in that live bath,
Each fish, which every channell hath,
Will amorously to thee swimme,
Gladder to catch thee, then thou him.

If thou, to be so seene, beest loath,
By Sunne, or Moone, thou darknest both,
And if my selfe have leave to see,
I need not their light, having thee.

Let others freeze with angling reeds,
And cut their legges, with shells and weeds,
Or treacherously poore fish beset,
With strangling snare, or windowie net:

Let coarse bold hands, from slimy nest
The bedded fish in banks out-wrest,
Or curious traitors, sleavesilke flies
Bewitch poore fishes wandring eyes.

For thee, thou needst no such deceit,
For thou thy selfe art thine owne bait;
That fish, that is not catch'd thereby,
Alas, is wiser farre then I.

The Blossome

    Little think'st thou, poore flower,
    Whom I have watch'd sixe or seaven dayes,
And seene thy birth, and seene what every houre
Gave to thy growth, thee to this height to raise,
And now dost laugh and triumph on this bough,
        Little think'st thou
That it will freeze anon, and that I shall
To morrow finde thee falne, or not at all.

    Little think'st thou poore heart
    That labour'st yet to nestle thee,
And think'st by hovering here to get a part
In a forbidden or forbidding tree,
And hop'st her stiffenesse by long siege to bow:
        Little think'st thou,
That thou to morrow, ere that Sunne doth wake,
Must with this Sunne, and mee a journey take.

    But thou which lov'st to bee
    Subtile to plague thy selfe, wilt say,
Alas, if you must goe, what's that to mee?
Here lyes my businesse, and here I will stay:
You goe to friends, whose love and meanes present
        Various content
To your eyes, eares, and tongue, and every part.
If then your body goe, what need you a heart?

    Well then, stay here; but know,
    When thou hast stayd and done thy most;
A naked thinking heart, that makes no show,
Is to a woman, but a kinde of Ghost;
How shall shee know my heart; or having none,
        Know thee for one?
Practise may make her know some other part,
But take my word, shee doth not know a Heart.

Meet mee at London, then,
 Twenty dayes hence, and thou shalt see
Mee fresher, and more fat, by being with men,
Then if I had staid still with her and thee.
For Gods sake, if you can, be you so too:
   I would give you
There, to another friend, whom wee shall finde
As glad to have my body, as my minde.

The Bracelet

Upon the losse of his Mistresses Chaine, for which
he made satisfaction

Not that in colour it was like thy haire,
For Armelets of that thou maist let me weare:
Nor that thy hand it oft embrac'd and kist,
For so it had that good, which oft I mist:
Nor for that silly old moralitie,
That as these linkes were knit, our love should bee:
Mourne I that I thy seavenfold chaine have lost;
Nor for the luck sake; but the bitter cost.
O, shall twelve righteous Angels, which as yet
No leaven of vile soder did admit;
Nor yet by any way have straid or gone
From the first state of their Creation;
Angels, which heaven commanded to provide
All things to me, and be my faithfull guide;
To gaine new friends, t'appease great enemies;
To comfort my soule, when I lie or rise;
Shall these twelve innocents, by thy severe
Sentence (dread judge) my sins great burden beare?
Shall they be damn'd, and in the furnace throwne,
And punisht for offences not their owne?
They save not me, they doe not ease my paines,
When in that hell they'are burnt and tyed in chains.
Were they but Crownes of France, I cared not,
For, most of these, their naturall Countreys rot
I think possesseth, they come here to us,
So pale, so lame, so leane, so ruinous;
And howsoe'r French Kings most Christian be,
Their Crownes are circumcis'd most Jewishly.
Or were they Spanish Stamps, still travelling,
That are become as Catholique as their King,
Those unlickt beare-whelps, unfil'd pistolets

That (more than Canon shot) availes or lets;
Which negligently left unrounded, looke
Like many angled figures, in the booke
Of some great Conjurer that would enforce
Nature, as these doe justice, from her course;
Which, as the soule quickens head, feet and heart,
As streames, like veines, run through th'earth's every part,
Visit all Countries, and have slily made
Gorgeous *France*, ruin'd, ragged and decay'd;
Scotland, which knew no State, proud in one day:
And mangled seventeen-headed *Belgia*.
Or were it such gold as that wherewithall
Almighty *Chymiques* from each minerall,
Having by subtle fire a soule out-pull'd;
Are dirtely and desperately gull'd:
I would not spit to quench the fire they'are in,
For, they are guilty of much hainous Sin.
But, shall my harmlesse angels perish? Shall
I lose my guard, my ease, my food, my all?
Much hope which they should nourish will be dead,
Much of my able youth, and lustyhead
Will vanish; if thou love let them alone,
For thou will love me lesse when they are gone;
And be content that some lowd squeaking Cryer
Well-pleas'd with one leane thred-bare groat, for hire,
May like a devill roare through every street;
And gall the finders conscience, if they meet.
Or let mee creepe to some dread Conjurer,
That with phantastique scheames fils full much paper;
Which hath divided heaven in tenements,
And with whores, theeves, and murderers stuft his rents,
So full, that though hee passe them all in sinne,
He leaves himselfe no roome to enter in.
But if, when all his art and time is spent,
Hee say 'twill ne'r be found; yet be content;
Receive from him that doome ungrudgingly,

Because he is the mouth of destiny.
    Thou say'st (alas) the gold doth still remaine,
Though it be chang'd, and put into a chaine;
So in the first falne angels, resteth still
Wisdome and knowledge; but, 'tis turn'd to ill:
As these should doe good works; and should provide
Necessities; but now must nurse thy pride.
And they are still bad angels; Mine are none;
For, forme gives being, and their forme is gone:
Pitty these Angels; yet their dignities
Passe Vertues, Powers, and Principalities.
    But, thou art resolute; Thy will be done!
Yet with such anguish, as her onely sonne
The Mother in the hungry grave doth lay,
Vnto the fire these Martyrs I betray.
Good soules, (for you give life to every thing)
Good Angels, (for good messages you bring)
Destin'd you might have beene to such an one,
As would have lov'd and worship'd you alone:
One that would suffer hunger, nakednesse,
Yea death, ere he would make your number lesse.
But, I am guilty of your sad decay;
May your few fellowes longer with me stay.
    But ô thou wretched finder whom I hate
So, that I almost pitty thy estate:
Gold being the heaviest metal amongst all,
May my most heavy curse upon thee fall:
Here fetter'd, manacled, and hang'd in chains,
First mayst thou bee; then chaind to hellish paines;
Or be with forraine gold brib'd to betray
Thy Countrey, and faile both of that and thy pay.
May the next thing thou stoop'st to reach, containe
Poyson, whose nimble fume rot thy moist braine;
Or libels, or some interdicted thing,
Which negligently kept, thy ruine bring.
Lust-bred diseases rot thee; and dwell with thee

Itching desire, and no abilitie.
May all the evils that gold ever wrought;
All mischiefes that all devils ever thought;
Want after plenty; poore and gouty age;
The plagues of travellers; love; marriage
Afflict thee, and at thy lives last moment,
May thy swolne sinnes themselves to thee present.
　　But, I forgive; repent thee honest man:
Gold is Restorative, restore it then:
But if from it thou beest loath to depart,
Because 'tis cordiali, would twere at thy heart.

Breake of Day

'Tis true, 'tis day; what though it be?
O wilt thou therefore rise from me?
Why should we rise, because 'tis light?
Did we lie downe, because 'twas night?
Love which in spight of darknesse brought us hether,
Should in despight of light keepe us together.

Light hath no tongue, but is all eye;
If it could speake as well as spie,
This were the worst, that it could say,
That being well, I faine would stay,
And that I lov'd my heart and honor so,
That I would not from him, that had them, goe.

Must businesse thee from hence remove?
Oh, that's the worst disease of love,
The poore, the foule, the false, love can
Admit, but not the busied man.
He which hath businesse, and makes love, doth doe
Such wrong, as when a maryed man doth wooe.

The Broken Heart

He is starke mad, who ever sayes,
   That he hath beene in love an houre,
Yet not that love so soone decayes,
   But that it can tenne in lesse space devour;
Who will beleeve mee, if I sweare
That I have had the plague a yeare?
   Who would not laugh at mee, if I should say,
   I saw a flaske of *powder burne a day?*

Ah, what a trifle is a heart,
   If once into loves hands it come!
All other griefes allow a part
   To other griefes, and aske themselves but some;
They come to us, but us Love draws,
Hee swallows us, and never chawes:
   By him, as by chain'd shot, whole rankes doe dye,
   He is the tyran Pike, our hearts the Frye.

If 'twere not so, what did become
   Of my heart, when I first saw thee?
I brought a heart into the roome,
   But from the roome, I carried none with mee:
If it had gone to thee, I know
Mine would have taught thine heart to show
   More pitty unto mee: but Love, alas,
   At one first blow did shiver it as glasse.

Yet nothing can to nothing fall,
   Nor any place be empty quite,
Therefore I thinke my breast hath all
   Those peeces still, though they be not unite;
And now as broken glasses show
A hundred lesser faces, so
   My ragges of heart can like, wish, and adore,
   But after one such love, can love no more.

A Burnt Ship

Out of a fired ship, which, by no way
But drowning, could be rescued from the flame,
Some men leap'd forth, and ever as they came
Neere the foes ships, did by their shot decay;
So all were lost, which in the ship were found,
     They in the sea being burnt, they in the burnt ship drown'd.

The Canonization

For Godsake hold your tongue, and let me love,
    Or chide my palsie, or my gout,
My five gray haires, or ruin'd fortune flout,
    With wealth your state, your minde with Arts improve,
        Take you a course, get you a place,
        Observe his honour, or his grace,
Or the Kings reall, or his stamped face
    Contemplate, what you will, approve,
    So you will let me love.

Alas, alas, who's injur'd by my love?
    What merchants ships have my sighs drown'd?
Who saies my teares have overflow'd his ground?
    When did my colds a forward spring remove?
        When did the heats which my veines fill
        Adde one more to the plaguie Bill?
Soldiers finde warres, and Lawyers finde out still
    Litigious men, which quarrels move,
    Though she and I do love.

Call us what you will, wee are made such by love;
    Call her one, mee another flye,
We'are Tapers too, and at our owne cost die,
    And wee in us finde the'Eagle and the Dove.
        The Phœnix ridle hath more wit
        By us, we two being one, are it.
So to one neutrall thing both sexes fit,
    Wee dye and rise the same, and prove
    Mysterious by this love.

Wee can dye by it, if not live by love,
    And if unfit for tombes and hearse
Our legend bee, it will be fit for verse;
    And if no peece of Chronicle wee prove,
        We'll build in sonnets pretty roomes;
        As well a well wrought urne becomes
The greatest ashes, as halfe-acre tombes,
    And by these hymnes, all shall approve
    Us *Canoniz'd* for Love:

And thus invoke us; You whom reverend love
    Made one anothers hermitage;
You, to whom love was peace, that now is rage;
    Who did the whole worlds soule contract, and drove
        Into the glasses of your eyes
        So made such mirrors, and such spies,
That they did all to you epitomize,
    Countries, Townes, Courts: Beg from above
    A patterne of your love!

Although thy hand and faith, and good workes too,
Have seal'd thy love which nothing should undoe
Yea though thou fall backe, that apostasie
Confirme thy love; yet much, much I feare thee.
Women are like the Arts, forc'd unto none,
Open to'all searchers, unpriz'd, if unknowne.
If I have caught a bird, and let him flie,
Another fouler using these meanes, as I,
May catch the same bird; and, as these things bee,
Women are made for men, not him, nor mee.
Foxes and goats; all beasts change when they please,
Shall women, more hot, wily, wild then these,
Be bound to one man, and did Nature then
Idly make them apter to'endure then men?
They'are our clogges, not their owne; if a man bee
Chain'd to a galley, yet the galley'is free;
Who hath a plow-land, casts all his seed corne there,
And yet allowes his ground more corne should beare;
Though Danuby into the sea must flow,
The sea receives the Rhene, Volga, and Po.
By nature, which gave it, this liberty
Thou lov'st, but Oh! canst thou love it and mee?
Likenesse glues love: and if that thou so doe,
To make us like and love, must I change too?
More then thy hate, I hate'it, rather let mee
Allow her change, then change as oft as shee,
And soe not teach, but force my'opinion
To love not any one, nor every one.
To live in one land, is captivitie,
To runne all countries, a wild roguery;
Waters stincke soone, if in one place they bide,
And in the vast sea are more putrifi'd:
But when they kisse one banke, and leaving this

Never looke backe, but the next banke doe kisse,
Then are they purest; Change'is the nursery
Of musicke, joy, life, and eternity.

Communitie

God wee must love, and must hate ill,
For ill is ill, and good good still,
   But there are things indifferent,
Which wee may neither hate, nor love,
But one, and then another prove,
   As wee shall finde our fancy bent.

If then at first wise Nature had
Made women either good or bad,
   Then some wee might hate, and some chuse,
But since shee did them so create,
That we may neither love, nor hate,
   Onely this rests, All, all may use.

If they were good it would be seene,
Good is as visible as greene,
   And to all eyes it selfe betrayes:
If they were bad, they could not last,
Bad doth it selfe, and others wast,
   So, they deserve nor blame, nor praise.

But they are ours as fruits are ours,
He that but tasts, he that devours,
   And he that leaves all, doth as well:
Chang'd loves are but chang'd sorts of meat,
And when hee hath the kernell eate,
   Who doth not fling away the shell?

ELEGIE VIII The Comparison

As the sweet sweat of Roses in a Still,
As that which from chaf'd muskats pores doth trill,
As the Almighty Balme of th'early East,
Such are the sweat drops of my Mistris breast,
And on her necke her skin such lustre sets,
They seeme no sweat drops, but pearle coronets.
Ranke sweaty froth thy Mistresse's brow defiles,
Like spermatique issue of ripe menstruous boiles,
Or like the skumme, which, by needs lawlesse law
Enforc'd, Sanserra's starved men did draw
From parboild shooes, and bootes, and all the rest
Which were with any soveraigne fatnes blest,
And like vile lying stones in saffrond tinne,
Or warts, or wheales, they hang upon her skinne.
Round as the world's her head, on every side,
Like to the fatall Ball which fell on Ide,
Or that whereof God had such jealousie,
As, for the ravishing thereof we die.
Thy *head* is like a rough-hewne statue of jeat,
Where marks for eyes, nose, mouth, are yet scarce set;
Like the first Chaos, or flat seeming face
Of Cynthia, when th'earths shadowes her embrace.
Like Proserpines white beauty-keeping chest,
Or Joves best fortunes urne, is her faire brest.
Thine's like worme eaten trunkes, cloth'd in seals skin,
Or grave, that's dust without, and stinke within.
And like that slender stalke, at whose end stands
The wood-bine quivering, are her armes and hands.
Like rough bark'd elmboughes, or the russet skin
Of men late scurg'd for madnes, or for sinne,
Like Sun-parch'd quarters on the citie gate,
Such is thy tann'd skins lamentable state.
And like a bunch of ragged carrets stand

The short swolne fingers of thy gouty hand.
Then like the Chymicks masculine equall fire,
Which in the Lymbecks warme wombe doth inspire
Into th'earths worthlesse durt a soule of gold,
Such cherishing heat her best lov'd part doth hold.
Thine's like the dread mouth of a fired gunne,
Or like hot liquid metalls newly runne
Into clay moulds, or like to that Ætna
Where round about the grasse is burnt away.
Are not your kisses then as filthy, and more,
As a worme sucking an invenom'd sore?
Doth not thy fearefull hand in feeling quake,
As one which gath'ring flowers, still feares a snake?
Is not your last act harsh, and violent,
As when a Plough a stony ground doth rent?
So kisse good Turtles, so devoutly nice
Are Priests in handling reverent sacrifice,
And such in searching wounds the Surgeon is
As wee, when wee embrace, or touch, or kisse.
Leave her, and I will leave comparing thus,
She, and comparisons are odious.

The Computation

For the first twenty yeares, since yesterday,
   I scarce beleev'd, thou could'st be gone away,
For forty more, I fed on favours past,
   And forty'on hopes, that thou would'st, they might last.
Teares drown'd one hundred, and sighes blew out two,
   A thousand, I did neither thinke, nor doe,
   Or not divide, all being one thought of you;
   Or in a thousand more, forgot that too.
Yet call not this long life; But thinke that I
Am, by being dead, Immortall; Can ghosts die?

Confined Love

Some man unworthy to be possessor
Of old or new love, himselfe being false or weake,
Thought his paine and shame would be lesser,
If on womankind he might his anger wreake,
And thence a law did grow,
One might but one man know;
But are other creatures so?

Are Sunne, Moone, or Starres by law forbidden,
To smile where they list, or lend away their light?
Are birds divorc'd, or are they chidden
If they leave their mate, or lie abroad a night?
Beasts doe no joyntures lose
Though they new lovers choose,
But we are made worse then those.

Who e'r rigg'd faire ship to lie in harbors,
And not to seeke new lands, or not to deale withall?
Or built faire houses, set trees, and arbors,
Only to lock up, or else to let them fall?
Good is not good, unlesse
A thousand it possesse,
But doth wast with greedinesse.

The Curse

Who ever guesses, thinks, or dreames he knowes
Who is my mistris, wither by this curse;
      His only, and only his purse
      May some dull heart to love dispose,
And shee yeeld then to all that are his foes;
  May he be scorn'd by one, whom all else scorne,
  Forsweare to others, what to her he'hath sworne,
  With feare of missing, shame of getting, torne:

Madnesse his sorrow, gout his cramp, may hee
Make, by but thinking, who hath made him such:
      And may he feele no touch
      Of conscience, but of fame, and bee
Anguish'd, not that 'twas sinne, but that 'twas shee:
  In early and long scarcenesse may he rot,
  For land which had been his, if he had not
  Himselfe incestuously an heire begot:

May he dreame Treason, and beleeve, that hee
Meant to performe it, and confesse, and die,
      And no record tell why:
      His sonnes, which none of his may bee,
Inherite nothing but his infamie:
  Or may he so long Parasites have fed,
  That he would faine be theirs, whom he hath bred,
  And at the last be circumcis'd for bread:

The venom of all stepdames, gamsters gall,
What Tyrans, and their subjects interwish,
      What Plants, Mynes, Beasts, Foule, Fish,
      Can contribute, all ill which all
Prophets, or Poets spake; And all which shall
  Be annex'd in schedules unto this by mee,
  Fall on that man; For if it be a shee
  Nature before hand hath out-cursed mee.

The Dampe

When I am dead, and Doctors know not why,
    And my friends curiositie
Will have me cut up to survay each part,
When they shall finde your Picture in my heart,
      You thinke a sodaine dampe of love
      Will through all their senses move,
And worke on them as mee, and so preferre
Your murder, to the name of Massacre.

Poore victories! But if you dare be brave,
    And pleasure in your conquest have,
First kill th'enormous Gyant, your *Disdaine,*
And let th'enchantresse *Honor,* next be slaine,
      And like a Goth and Vandall rize,
      Deface Records, and Histories
Of your owne arts and triumphs over men,
And without such advantage kill me then.

For I could muster up as well as you
    My Gyants, and my Witches too,
Which are vast *Constancy,* and *Secretnesse,*
But these I neyther looke for, nor professe;
      Kill mee as Woman, let mee die
      As a meere man; doe you but try
Your passive valor, and you shall finde than,
In that you'have odds enough of any man.

The Dissolution

Shee'is dead; And all which die
To their first Elements resolve;
And wee were mutuall Elements to us,
    And made of one another.
My body then doth hers involve,
And those things whereof I consist, hereby
In me abundant grow, and burdenous,
    And nourish not, but smother.
My fire of Passion, sighes of ayre,
Water of teares, and earthly sad despaire,
    Which my materialls bee,
But neere worne out by loves securitie,
Shee, to my losse, doth by her death repaire,
   And I might live long wretched so
But that my fire doth with my fuell grow.
    Now as those Active Kings
  Whose foraine conquest treasure brings,
Receive more, and spend more, and soonest breake:
This (which I am amaz'd that I can speake)
    This death, hath with my store
     My use encreas'd.
And so my soule more earnestly releas'd,
Will outstrip hers; As bullets flowen before
A latter bullet may o'rtake, the pouder being more.

ELEGIE X The Dreame

Image of her whom I love, more then she,
    Whose faire impression in my faithfull heart,
Makes mee her *Medall,* and makes her love mee,
    As Kings do coynes, to which their stamps impart
The value: goe, and take my heart from hence,
    Which now is growne too great and good for me:
Honours oppresse weake spirits, and our sense
    Strong objects dull; the more, the lesse wee see.
When you are gone, and *Reason* gone with you,
    Then *Fantasie* is Queene and Soule, and all;
She can present joyes meaner then you do;
    Convenient, and more proportionall.
So, if I dreame I have you, I have you,
    For, all our joyes are but fantasticall.
And so I scape the paine, for paine is true;
    And sleepe which locks up sense, doth lock out all.
After a such fruition I shall wake,
    And, but the waking, nothing shall repent;
And shall to love more thankfull Sonnets make,
    Then if more *honour, teares,* and *paines* were spent.
But dearest heart, and dearer image stay;
    Alas, true joyes at best are *dreame* enough;
Though you stay here you passe too fast away:
    For even at first lifes *Taper* is a snuffe.
Fill'd with her love, may I be rather grown
Mad with much *heart,* then *ideott* with none.

The Extasie

Where, like a pillow on a bed,
   A Pregnant banke swel'd up, to rest
The violets reclining head,
   Sat we two, one anothers best.
Our hands were firmely cimented
   With a fast balme, which thence did spring,
Our eye-beames twisted, and did thred
   Our eyes, upon one double string;
So to'entergraft our hands, as yet
   Was all the meanes to make us one,
And pictures in our eyes to get
   Was all our propagation.
As 'twixt two equal Armies, Fate
   Suspends uncertaine victorie,
Our soules, (which to advance their state,
   Were gone out,) hung 'twixt her, and mee.
And whil'st our soules negotiate there,
   Wee like sepulchrall statues lay;
All day, the same our postures were,
   And wee said nothing, all the day.
If any, so by love refin'd,
   That he soules language understood,
And by good love were growen all minde,
   Within convenient distance stood,
He (though he knew not which soule spake,
   Because both meant, both spake the same)
Might thence a new concoction take,
   And part farre purer then he came.
This Extasie doth unperplex
   (We said) and tell us what we love,
Wee see by this, it was not sexe,
   Wee see, we saw not what did move:
But as all severall soules containe

Mixture of things, they know not what,
Love, these mixt soules doth mixe againe,
    And makes both one, each this and that.
A single violet transplant,
    The strength, the colour, and the size,
(All which before was poore, and scant,)
    Redoubles still, and multiplies.
When love, with one another so
    Interinanimates two soules,
That abler soule, which thence doth flow,
    Defects of lonelinesse controules.
Wee then, who are this new soule, know,
    Of what we are compos'd, and made,
For, th'Atomies of which we grow,
    Are soules, whom no change can invade.
But O alas, so long, so farre
    Our bodies why doe wee forbeare?
They'are ours, though they'are not wee, Wee are
    The intelligences, they the spheare.
We owe them thankes, because they thus,
    Did us, to us, at first convay,
Yeelded their forces, sense, to us,
    Nor are drosse to us, but allay.
On man heavens influence workes not so,
    But that it first imprints the ayre,
Soe soule into the soule may flow,
    Though it to body first repaire.
As our blood labours to beget
    Spirits, as like soules as it can,
Because such fingers need to knit
    That subtile knot, which makes us man:
So must pure lovers soules descend
    T'affections, and to faculties,
Which sense may reach and apprehend,
    Else a great Prince in prison lies.
To'our bodies turne wee then, that so

Weake men on love reveal'd may looke;
Loves mysteries in soules doe grow,
   But yet the body is his booke.
And if some lover, such as wee,
   Have heard this dialogue of one,
Let him still marke us, he shall see
   Small change, when we'are to bodies gone.

The Expiration

So, so, breake off this last lamenting kisse,
    Which sucks two soules, and vapors Both away,
Turne thou ghost that way, and let mee turne this,
    And let our selves benight our happiest day,
We ask'd none leave to love; nor will we owe
    Any, so cheape a death, as saying, Goe;

Goe; and if that word have not quite kil'd thee,
    Ease mee with death, by bidding mee goe too.
Or, if it have, let my word worke on mee,
    And a just office on a murderer doe.
Except it be too late, to kill me so,
    Being double dead, going, and bidding, goe.

Farewell to Love

  Whilst yet to prove,
I thought there was some Deitie in love
  So did I reverence, and gave
Worship, as Atheists at their dying houre
Call, what they cannot name, an unknowne power,
  As ignorantly did I crave:
    Thus when
Things not yet knowne are coveted by men,
  Our desires give them fashion, and so
As they waxe lesser, fall, as they sise, grow.

  But, from late faire
His highnesse sitting in a golden Chaire,
  Is not lesse cared for after three dayes
By children, then the thing which lovers so
Blindly admire, and with such worship wooe;
  Being had, enjoying it decayes:
    And thence,
What before pleas'd them all, takes but one sense,
  And that so lamely, as it leaves behinde
A kinde of sorrowing dulnesse to the minde.

  Ah cannot wee,
As well as Cocks and Lyons jocund be,
  After such pleasures? Unlesse wise
Nature decreed (since each such Act, they say,
Diminisheth the length of life a day)
  This, as shee would man should despise
    The sport;
Because that other curse of being short,
  And onely for a minute made to be,
Eager, desires to raise posterity.

   Since so, my minde
Shall not desire what no man else can finde,
  I'll no more dote and runne
To pursue things which had indammag'd me.
And when I come where moving beauties be,
  As men doe when the summers Sunne
    Growes great,
Though I admire their greatnesse, shun their heat;
  Each place can afford shadowes. If all faile,
'Tis but applying worme-seed to the Taile.

A Feaver

Oh doe not die, for I shall hate
　　All women so, when thou art gone,
That thee I shall not celebrate,
　　When I remember, thou wast one.

But yet thou canst not die, I know;
　　To leave this world behinde, is death,
But when thou from this world wilt goe,
　　The whole world vapors with thy breath.

Or if, when thou, the worlds soule, goest,
　　It stay, 'tis but thy carkasse then,
The fairest woman, but thy ghost,
　　But corrupt wormes, the worthyest men.

O wrangling schooles, that search what fire
　　Shall burne this world, had none the wit
Unto this knowledge to aspire,
　　That this her feaver might be it?

And yet she cannot wast by this,
　　Nor long beare this torturing wrong,
For much corruption needfull is
　　To fuell such a feaver long.

These burning fits but meteors bee,
　　Whose matter in thee is soone spent.
Thy beauty, 'and all parts, which are thee,
　　Are unchangeable firmament.

Yet t'was of my minde, seising thee,
　　Though it in thee cannot persever.
For I had rather owner bee
　　Of thee one houre, then all else ever.

The Flea

Marke but this flea, and marke in this,
How little that which thou deny'st me is;
It suck'd me first, and now sucks thee,
And in this flea, our two bloods mingled bee;
Thou know'st that this cannot be said
A sinne, nor shame, nor losse of maidenhead,
   Yet this enjoyes before it wooe,
    And pamper'd swells with one blood made of two,
    And this, alas, is more then wee would doe.

Oh stay, three lives in one flea spare,
Where wee almost, yea more then maryed are,
This flea is you and I, and this
Our mariage bed, and mariage temple is;
Though parents grudge, and you, w'are met,
And cloysterd in these living walls of Jet.
   Though use make you apt to kill mee,
    Let not to that, selfe murder added bee,
    And sacrilege, three sinnes in killing three.

Cruell and sodaine, hast thou since
Purpled thy naile, in blood of innocence?
Wherein could this flea guilty bee,
Except in that drop which it suckt from thee?
Yet thou triumph'st, and saist that thou
Find'st not thy selfe, nor mee the weaker now;
   'Tis true, then learne how false, feares bee;
    Just so much honor, when thou yeeld'st to mee,
    Will wast, as this flea's death tooke life from thee.

The Funerall

Who ever comes to shroud me, do not harme
     Nor question much
That subtile wreath of haire, which crowns my arme;
The mystery, the signe you must not touch,
     For 'tis my outward Soule,
Viceroy to that, which then to heaven being gone,
     Will leave this to controule,
And keepe these limbes, her Provinces, from dissolution.

For if the sinewie thread my braine lets fall
     Through every part,
Can tye those parts, and make mee one of all;
These haires which upward grew, and strength and art
     Have from a better braine,
Can better do'it; Except she meant that I
     By this should know my pain,
As prisoners then are manacled, when they'are condemn'd to die.

What ere shee meant by'it, bury it with me,
     For since I am
Loves martyr, it might breed idolatrie,
If into others hands these Reliques came;
     As 'twas humility
To afford to it all that a Soule can doe,
     So, 'tis some bravery,
That since you would save none of mee, I bury some of you.

Song

Goe, and catche a falling starre,
　　Get with child a mandrake roote,
Tell me, where all past yeares are,
　　Or who cleft the Divels foot,
Teach me to heare Mermaides singing,
Or to keep off envies stinging,
　　　　And finde
　　　　What winde
Serves to advance an honest minde.

If thou beest borne to strange sights,
　　Things invisible to see,
Ride ten thousand daies and nights,
　　Till age snow white haires on thee,
Thou, when thou retorn'st, wilt tell mee
All strange wonders that befell thee,
　　　　And sweare
　　　　No where
Lives a woman true, and faire.

If thou findst one, let mee know,
　　Such a Pilgrimage were sweets;
Yet doe not, I would not goe,
　　Though at next doore wee might meet,
Though shee were true, when you met her,
And last, till you write your letter,
　　　　Yet shee
　　　　Will bee
Falfe, ere I come, to two, or three.

Goodfriday 1613

Made as I was riding Westward that day

Let mans Soule be a Spheare, and then, in this,
The intelligence that moves, devotion is,
And as the other Spheares, by being growne
Subject to forraigne motions, lose their owne,
And being by others hurried every day,
Scarce in a yeare their naturall forme obey:
Pleasure or businesse, so, our Soules admit
For their first mover, and are whirld by it.
Hence is't, that I am carryed towards the West
This day, when my Soules forme bends toward the East.
There I should see a Sunne, by rising set,
And by that setting endlesse day beget;
But that Christ on this Crosse, did rise and fall,
Sinne had eternally benighted all.
Yet dare I'almost be glad, I do not see
That spectacle of too much weight for mee.
Who sees Gods face, that is selfe life, must dye;
What a death were it then to see God dye?
It made his owne Lieutenant Nature shrinke,
It made his footstoole crack, and the Sunne winke.
Could I behold those hands which span the Poles,
And turne all spheares at once, peirc'd with those holes?
Could I behold that endlesse height which is
Zenith to us, and our Antipodes,
Humbled below us? or that blood which is
The seat of all our Soules, if not of his,
Made durt of dust, or that flesh which was worne
By God, for his apparell, rag'd, and torne?
If on these things I durst not looke, durst I
Upon his miserable mother cast mine eye,
Who was Gods partner here, and furnish'd thus

Halfe of that Sacrifice, which ransom'd us?
Though these things, as I ride, be from mine eye,
They'are present yet unto my memory,
For that looks towards them; and thou look'st towards mee,
O Saviour, as thou hang'st upon the tree;
I turne my backe to thee, but to receive
Corrections, till thy mercies bid thee leave.
O thinke mee worth thine anger, punish mee,
Burne off my rusts, and my deformity,
Restore thine Image, so much, by thy grace,
That thou may'st know mee, and I'll turne my face.

The Good-Morrow

I wonder by my troth, what thou, and I
Did, till we lov'd? were we not wean'd till then?
But suck'd on countrey pleasures, childishly?
Or snorted we in the seaven sleepers den?
T'was so; But this, all pleasures fancies bee.
If ever any beauty I did see,
Which I desir'd, and got, t'was but a dreame of thee.

And now good morrow to our waking soules,
Which watch not one another out of feare;
For love, all love of other sights controules,
And makes one little roome, an every where.
Let sea-discoverers to new worlds have gone,
Let Maps to other, worlds on worlds have showne,
Let us possesse one world, each hath one, and is one.

My face in thine eye, thine in mine appeares,
And true plain hearts doe in the faces rest,
Where can we finde two better hemispheares
Without sharpe North, without declining West?
What ever dyes, was not mixt equally;
If our two loves be one, or, thou and I
Love so alike, that none doe slacken, none can die.

ELEGIE V His Picture

Here take my Picture; though I bid farewell,
Thine, in my heart, where my soule dwels, shall dwell.
'Tis like me now, but I dead, 'twill be more
When wee are shadowes both, then 'twas before.
When weather-beaten I come backe; my hand,
Perhaps with rude oares torne, or Sun beams tann'd,
My face and brest of hairecloth, and my head
With cares rash sodaine stormes, being o'rspread,
My body'a sack of bones, broken within,
And powders blew staines scatter'd on my skinne;
If rivall fooles taxe thee to'have lov'd a man,
So foule, and course, as, Oh, I may seeme than,
This shall say what I was: and thou shalt say,
Doe his hurts reach mee? doth my worth decay?
Or doe they reach his judging minde, that hee
Should now love lesse, what hee did love to see?
That which in him was faire and delicate,
Was but the milke, which in loves childish state
Did nurse it: who now is growne strong enough
To feed on that, which to disused tasts seemes tough.

Holy Sonnets

I

Thou hast made me, And shall thy worke decay?
Repaire me now, for now mine end doth haste,
I runne to death, and death meets me as fast,
And all my pleasures are like yesterday;
I dare not move my dimme eyes any way,
Despaire behind, and death before doth cast
Such terrour, and my feeble flesh doth waste
By sinne in it, which it t'wards hell doth weigh;
Onely thou art above, and when towards thee
By thy leave I can looke, I rise againe;
But our old subtle foe so tempteth me,
That not one houre my selfe I can sustaine;
Thy Grace may wing me to prevent his art,
And thou like Adamant draw mine iron heart.

II

As due by many titles I resigne
My selfe to thee, O God, first I was made
By thee, and for thee, and when I was decay'd
Thy blood bought that, the which before was thine;
I am thy sonne, made with thy selfe to shine,
Thy servant, whose paines thou hast still repaid,
Thy sheepe, thine Image, and, till I betray'd
My selfe, a temple of thy Spirit divine;
Why doth the devill then usurpe on mee?
Why doth he steale, nay ravish that's thy right?
Except thou rise and for thine owne worke fight,
Oh I shall soone despaire, when I doe see
That thou lov'st mankind well, yet wilt'not chuse me.
And Satan hates mee, yet is loth to lose mee.

III

O might those sighes and teares returne againe
Into my breast and eyes, which I have spent,
That I might in this holy discontent
Mourne with some fruit, as I have mourn'd in vaine;
In mine Idolatry what showres of raine
Mine eyes did waste? what griefs my heart did rent?
That sufferance was my sinne; now I repent;
'Cause I did suffer I must suffer paine.
Th'hydroptique drunkard, and night-scouting thiefe,
The itchy Lecher, and selfe tickling proud
Have the remembrance of past joyes, for reliefe
Of comming ills. To (poore) me is allow'd
No ease; for, long, yet vehement griefe hath beene
Th'effect and cause, the punishment and sinne.

IV

Oh my blacke Soule! now thou art summoned
By sicknesse, deaths herald, and champion;
Thou art like a pilgrim, which abroad hath done
Treason, and durst not turne to whence hee is fled,
Or like a thiefe, which till deaths doome be read,
Wisheth himselfe delivered from prison;
But damn'd and hal'd to execution,
Wisheth that still he might be imprisoned.
Yet grace, if thou repent, thou canst not lacke;
But who shall give thee that grace to beginne?
Oh make thy selfe with holy mourning blacke,
And red with blushing, as thou art with sinne;
Or wash thee in Christs blood, which hath this might
That being red, it dyes red soules to white.

V

I am a little world made cunningly
Of Elements, and an Angelike spright,
But black sinne hath betraid to endlesse night
My worlds both parts, and (oh) both parts must die.
You which beyond that heaven which was most high
Have found new sphears, and of new lands can write,
Powre new seas in mine eyes, that so I might
Drowne my world with my weeping earnestly,
Or wash it, if it must be drown'd no more:
But oh it must be burnt! alas the fire
Of lust and envie have burnt it heretofore,
And made it fouler; Let their flames retire,
And burne me ô Lord, with a fiery zeale
Of thee and thy house, which doth in eating heale.

VI

This is my playes last scene, here heavens appoint
My pilgrimages last mile; and my race
Idly, yet quickly runne, hath this last pace,
My spans last inch, my minutes latest point,
And gluttonous death, will instantly unjoynt
My body, and soule, and I shall sleepe a space,
But my'ever-waking part shall see that face,
Whose feare already shakes my every joynt:
Then, as my soule, to'heaven her first seate, takes flight,
And earth-borne body, in the earth shall dwell,
So, fall my sinnes, that all may have their right,
To where they'are bred, and would presse me, to hell.
Impute me righteous, thus purg'd of evill,
For thus I leave the world, the flesh, the devill.

VII

At the round earths imagin'd corners, blow
Your trumpets, Angells, and arise, arise
From death, you numberlesse infinities
Of soules, and to your scattred bodies goe,
All whom the flood did, and fire shall o'erthrow,
All whom warre, dearth, age, agues, tyrannies,
Despaire, law, chance, hath slaine, and you whose eyes,
Shall behold God, and never tast deaths woe.
But let them sleepe, Lord, and mee mourne a space,
For, if above all these, my sinnes abound,
'Tis late to aske abundance of thy grace,
When wee are there; here on this lowly ground,
Teach mee how to repent; for that's as good
As if thou'hadst seal'd my pardon, with thy blood.

VIII

If faithfull soules be alike glorifi'd
As Angels, then my fathers soule doth see,
And adds this even to full felicitie,
That valiantly I hels wide mouth o'rstride:
But if our mindes to these soules be descry'd
By circumstances, and by signes that be
Apparent in us, not immediately,
How shall my mindes white truth by them be try'd?
They see idolatrous lovers weepe and mourne,
And vile blasphemous Conjurers to call
On Jesus name, and Pharisaicall
Dissemblers feigne devotion. Then turne
O pensive soule, to God, for he knowes best
Thy true griefe, for he put it in my breast.

IX

If poysonous mineralls, and if that tree,
Whose fruit threw death on else immortall us,
If lecherous goats, if serpents envious
Cannot be damn'd; Alas; why should I bee?
Why should intent or reason, borne in mee,
Make sinnes, else equall, in mee more heinous?
And mercy being easie, and glorious
To God; in his sterne wrath, why threatens hee?
But who am I, that dare dispute with thee
O God? Oh! of thine onely worthy blood,
And my teares, make a heavenly Lethean flood,
And drowne in it my sinnes blacke memorie;
That thou remember them, some claime as debt,
I thinke it mercy, if thou wilt forget.

X

Death be not proud, though some have called thee
Mighty and dreadfull, for, thou art not soe,
For, those, whom thou think'st, thou dost overthrow,
Die not, poore death, nor yet canst thou kill mee.
From rest and sleepe, which but thy pictures bee,
Much pleasure, then from thee, much more must flow,
And soonest our best men with thee doe goe,
Rest of their bones, and soules deliverie.
Thou art slave to Fate, Chance, kings, and desperate men,
And dost with poyson, warre, and sicknesse dwell,
And poppie, or charmes can make us sleepe as well,
And better then thy stroake; why swell'st thou then?
One short sleepe past, wee wake eternally,
And death shall be no more; death, thou shalt die.

XI

Spit in my face you Jewes, and pierce my side,
Buffet, and scoffe, scourge, and crucifie mee,
For I have sinn'd, and sinn'd, and onely hee,
Who could do no iniquitie, hath dyed:
But by my death can not be satisfied
My sinnes, which passe the Jewes impiety:
They kill'd once an inglorious man, but I
Crucifie him daily, being now glorified.
Oh let mee then, his strange love still admire:
Kings pardon, but he bore our punishment.
And *Jacob* came cloth'd in vile harsh attire
But to supplant, and with gainfull intent:
God cloth'd himselfe in vile mans flesh, that so
Hee might be weake enough to suffer woe.

XII

Why are wee by all creatures waited on?
Why doe the prodigall elements supply
Life and food to mee, being more pure then I,
Simple, and further from corruption?
Why brook'st thou, ignorant horse, subjection?
Why dost thou bull, and bore so seelily
Dissemble weaknesse, and by'one mans stroke die,
Whose whole kinde, you might swallow and feed upon?
Weaker I am, woe is mee, and worse then you,
You have not sinn'd, nor need be timorous.
But wonder at a greater wonder, for to us
Created nature doth these things subdue,
But their Creator, whom sin, nor nature tyed,
For us, his Creatures, and his foes, hath dyed.

The Indifferent

I Can love both faire and browne,
Her whom abundance melts, and her whom want betraies,
Her who loves lonenesse best, and her who maskes and plaies,
Her whom the country form'd, and whom the town,
Her who beleeves, and her who tries,
Her who still weepes with spungie eyes,
And her who is dry corke, and never cries;
I can love her, and her, and you and you,
I can love any, so she be not true.

Will no other vice content you?
Wil it not serve your turn to do, as did your mothers?
Or have you all old vices spent, and now would finde out others?
Or doth a feare, that men are true, torment you?
Oh we are not, be not you so,
Let mee, and doe you, twenty know.
Rob mee, but binde me not, and let me goe.
Must I, who came to travaile thorow you,
Grow your fixt subject, because you are true?

Venus heard me sigh this song,
And by Loves sweetest Part, Variety, she swore,
She heard not this till now; and that it should be so no more.
She went, examin'd, and return'd ere long,
And said, alas, Some two or three
Poore Heretiques in love there bee,
Which thinke to stablish dangerous constancie.
But I have told them, since you will be true,
You shall be true to them, who'are false to you.

ELEGIE I Jealosie

Fond woman, which would'st have thy husband die,
And yet complain'st of his great jealousie;
If swolne with poyson, hee lay in'his last bed,
His body with a sere-barke covered,
Drawing his breath, as thick and short, as can
The nimblest crocheting Musitian,
Ready with loathsome vomiting to spue
His Soule out of one hell, into a new,
Made deafe with his poore kindreds howling cries,
Begging with few feign'd teares, great legacies,
Thou would'st not weepe, but jolly, 'and frolicke bee,
As a slave, which to morrow should be free;
Yet weep'st thou, when thou seest him hungerly
Swallow his owne death, hearts-bane jealousie.
O give him many thanks, he'is courteous,
That in suspecting kindly warneth us.
Wee must not, as wee us'd, flout openly,
In scoffing ridles, his deformitie;
Nor at his boord together being satt,
With words, nor touch, scarce lookes adulterate.
Nor when he swolne, and pamper'd with great fare,
Sits downe, and snorts, cag'd in his basket chaire,
Must wee usurpe his owne bed any more,
Nor kisse and play in his house, as before.
Now I see many dangers; for that is
His realme, his castle, and his diocesse.
But if, as envious men, which would revile
Their Prince, or coyne his gold, themselves exile
Into another countrie, 'and doe it there,
Wee play'in another house, what should we feare?
There we will scorne his houshold policies,
His seely plots, and pensionary spies,
As the inhabitants of Thames right side
Do Londons Major; or Germans, the Popes pride.

A Lecture upon the Shadow

Stand still, and I will read to thee
A Lecture, Love, in loves philosophy.
    These three houres that we have spent,
    Walking here, Two shadowes went
Along with us, which we our selves produc'd;
But, now the Sunne is just above our head,
    We doe those shadowes tread;
    And to brave clearnesse all things are reduc'd.
  So whilst our infant loves did grow,
  Disguises did, and shadowes, flow,
  From us, and our cares; but, now 'tis not so.

That love hath not attain'd the high'st degree,
Which is still diligent lest others see.

Except our loves at this noone stay,
We shall new shadowes make the other way.
    As the first were made to blinde
    Others; these which come behinde
Will worke upon our selves, and blind our eyes.
If our loves faint, and westwardly decline;
    To me thou, falsly, thine,
    And I to thee mine actions shall disguise.
  The morning shadowes weare away,
  But these grow longer all the day,
  But oh, loves day is short, if love decay.

Love is a growing, or full constant light;
And his first minute, after noone, is night.

The Legacie

When I dyed last, and, Deare, I dye
   As often as from thee I goe,
   Though it be but an houre agoe,
And Lovers houres be full eternity,
I can remember yet, that I
   Something did say, and something did bestow;
Though I be dead, which sent mee, I should be
Mine owne executor and Legacie.

I heard mee say, Tell her anon,
   That my selfe, (that is you, not I,)
   Did kill me, and when I felt mee dye,
I bid mee send my heart, when I was gone,
But I alas could there finde none,
When I had ripp'd me,' and search'd where hearts lye;
   It kill'd mee againe, that I who still was true,
In life, in my last Will should cozen you.

Yet I found something like a heart,
   But colours it, and corners had,
   It was not good, it was not bad,
It was intire to none, and few had part.
As good as could be made by art
   It seem'd; and therefore for our losses sad,
I meant to send this heart in stead of mine,
But oh, no man could hold it, for twas thine.

Lovers Infinitenesse

If yet I have not all thy love,
Deare, I shall never have it all,
I cannot breath one other sigh, to move;
Nor can intreat one other teare to fall.
And all my treasure, which should purchase thee,
Sighs, teares, and oathes, and letters I have spent,
Yet no more can be due to mee,
Then at the bargaine made was ment,
If then thy gift of love were partiall,
That some to mee, some should to others fall,
  Deare, I shall never have Thee All.

Or if then thou gavest mee all,
All was but All, which thou hadst then,
But if in thy heart, since, there be or shall,
New love created bee, by other men,
Which have their stocks intire, and can in teares,
In sighs, in oathes, and letters outbid mee,
This new love may beget new feares,
For, this love was not vowed by thee.
And yet it was, thy gift being generall,
The ground, thy heart is mine, what ever shall
  Grow there, deare, I should have it all.

Yet I would not have all yet,
Hee that hath all can have no more,
And since my love doth every day admit
New growth, thou shouldst have new rewards in store;
Thou canst not every day give me thy heart,
If thou canst give it, then thou never gavest it:
Loves riddles are, that though thy heart depart,
It stayes at home, and thou with losing savest it:
But wee will have a way more liberall,
Then changing hearts, to joyne them, so wee shall
  Be one, and one anothers All.

Loves Alchymie

Some that have deeper digg'd loves Myne then I,
Say, where his centrique happinesse doth lie:
      I have lov'd, and got, and told,
But should I love, get, tell, till I were old,
I should not finde that hidden mysterie;
      Oh, 'tis imposture all:
And as no chymique yet th'Elixar got,
      But glorifies his pregnant pot,
      If by the way to him befall
Some odoriferous thing, or medicinall,
  So, lovers dreame a rich and long delight,
  But get a winter-seeming summers night.

Our ease, our thrift, our honor, and our day,
Shall we, for this vaine Bubles shadow pay?
      Ends love in this, that my man,
Can be as happy'as I can; If he can
Endure the short scorne of a Bridegroomes play?
      That loving wretch that sweares,
'Tis not the bodies marry, but the mindes,
      Which he in her Angelique findes,
      Would sweare as justly, that he heares,
In that dayes rude hoarse minstralsey, the spheares.
  Hope not for minde in women; at their best
  Sweetnesse and wit, they'are but *Mummy*, possest.

Loves Deitie

I long to talke with some old lovers ghost,
    Who dyed before the god of Love was borne:
I cannot thinke that hee, who then lov'd most,
    Sunke so low, as to love one which did scorne.
But since this god produc'd a destinie,
And that vice-nature, custome, lets it be;
    I must love her, that loves not mee.

Sure, they which made him god, meant not so much,
    Nor he, in his young godhead practis'd it;
But when an even flame two hearts did touch,
    His office was indulgently to fit
Actives to passives. Correspondencie
Only his subject was; It cannot bee
    Love, till I love her, that loves mee.

But every moderne god will now extend
    His vast prerogative, as far as Jove.
To rage, to lust, to write to, to commend,
    All is the purlewe of the God of Love.
Oh were wee wak'ned by this Tyrannie
To ungod this child againe, it could not bee
    I should love her, who loves not mee.

Rebell and Atheist too, why murmure I,
    As though I felt the worst that love could doe?
Love might make me leave loving, or might trie
    A deeper plague, to make her love me too,
Which, since she loves before, I'am loth to see;
Falshood is worse then hate; and that must bee,
    If shee whom I love, should love mee.

Loves Diet

To what a combersome unwieldinesse
And burdenous corpulence my love had growne,
   But that I did, to make it lesse,
   And keepe it in proportion,
Give it a diet, made it feed upon
That which love worst endures, *discretion*.

Above one sigh a day I'allow'd him not,
Of which my fortune, and my faults had part;
   And if sometimes by stealth he got
   A she sigh from my mistresse heart,
And thought to feast on that, I let him see
'Twas neither very sound, nor meant to mee.

If he wroung from mee'a teare, I brin'd it so
With scorne or shame, that him it nourish'd not;
   If he suck'd hers, I let him know
   'Twas not a teare, which hee had got,
His drinke was counterfeit, as was his meat;
For, eyes which rowle towards all, weepe not, but sweat.

What ever he would dictate, I writ that,
But burnt my letters; When she writ to me,
   And that that favour made him fat,
   I said, if any title bee
Convey'd by this, Ah, what doth it availe,
To be the fortieth name in an entaile?

Thus I reclaim'd my buzard love, to flye
At what, and when, and how, and where I chuse;
   Now negligent of sport I lye,
   And now as other Fawkners use,
I spring a mistresse, sweare, write, sigh and weepe:
And the game kill'd, or lost, goe talke, and sleepe.

Loves Exchange

Love, any devill else but you,
Would for a given Soule give something too.
At Court your fellowes every day,
Give th'art of Riming, Huntsmanship, or Play,
For them which were their owne before;
Onely I have nothing which gave more,
But am, alas, by being lowly, lower.

I aske no dispensation now
To falsifie a teare, or sigh, or vow,
I do not sue from thee to draw
A *non obstante* on natures law,
These are prerogatives, they inhere
In thee and thine; none should forsweare
Except that hee *Loves* minion were.

Give mee thy weaknesse, make mee blinde,
Both wayes, as thou and thine, in eies and minde;
Love, let me never know that this
Is love, or, that love childish is;
Let me not know that others know
That she knowes my paines, least that so
A tender shame make me mine owne new woe.

If thou give nothing, yet thou'art just,
Because I would not thy first motions trust;
Small townes which stand stiffe, till great shot
Enforce them, by warres law *condition* not.
Such in loves warfare is my case,
I may not article for grace,
Having put Love at last to shew this face.

This face, by which he could command
And change the Idolatrie of any land,
This face, which wheresoe'r it comes,
Can call vow'd men from cloisters, dead from tombes,
And melt both Poles at once, and store
Deserts with'cities, and make more
Mynes in the earth, then Quarries were before.

For this, Love is enrag'd with mee,
Yet kills not. If I must example bee
To future Rebells; If th'unborne
Must learne, by my being cut up, and torne:
Kill, and dissect me, Love; for this
Torture against thine owne end is,
Rack't carcasses make ill Anatomies.

Loves Growth

I scarce beleeve my love to be so pure
    As I had thought it was,
    Because it doth endure
Vicissitude, and season, as the grasse;
Me thinkes I lyed all winter, when I swore,
My love was infinite, if spring make'it more.

But if this medicine, love, which cures all sorrow
With more, not onely bee no quintessence,
But mixt of all stuffes, paining soule, or sense,
And of the Sunne his working vigour borrow,
Love's not so pure, and abstract, as they use
To say, which have no Mistresse but their Muse,
But as all else, being elemented too,
Love sometimes would contemplate, sometimes do.

And yet no greater, but more eminent,
    Love by the spring is growne;
    As, in the firmament,
Starres by the Sunne are not inlarg'd, but showne.
Gentle love deeds, as blossomes on a bough,
From loves awakened root do bud out now.

If, as in water stir'd more circles bee
Produc'd by one, love such additions take,
Those like so many spheares, but one heaven make,
For, they are all concentrique unto thee;
And though each spring doe adde to love new heate,
As princes doe in times of action get
New taxes, and remit them not in peace,
No winter shall abate the springs encrease.

ELEGIE XVIII Loves Progress

Who ever loves, if he do not propose
The right true end of love, he's one that goes
To sea for nothing but to make him sick:
Love is a bear-whelp born, if we o're lick
Our love, and force it new strange shapes to take,
We erre, and of a lump a monster make.
Were not a Calf a monster that were grown
Face'd like a man, though better then his own?
Perfection is in unitie: preferr
One woman first, and then one thing in her.
I, when I value gold, may think upon
The ductilness, the application,
The wholsomness, the ingenuitie,
From rust, from soil, from fire ever free:
But if I love it, 'tis because 'tis made
By our new nature (Use) the soul of trade.
    All these in women we might think upon
(If women had them) and yet love but one.
Can men more injure women then to say
They love them for that, by which they're not they?
Makes virtue woman? must I cool my bloud
Till I both be, and find one wise and good?
May barren Angels love so. But if we
Make love to woman; virtue is not she:
As beauty'is not nor wealth: He that strayes thus
From her to hers, is more adulterous,
Then if he took her maid. Search every spheare
And firmament, our *Cupid* is not there:
He's an infernal god and under ground,
With *Pluto* dwells, where gold and fire abound:
Men to such Gods, their sacrificing Coles
Did not in Altars lay, but pits and holes.
Although we see Celestial bodies move

Above the earth, the earth we Till and love:
So we her ayres contemplate, words and heart,
And virtues; but we love the Centrique part.
    Nor is the soul more worthy, or more fit
For love, then this, as infinite as it.
But in attaining this desired place
How much they erre; that set out at the face?
The hair a Forest is of Ambushes,
Of springes, snares, fetters and manacles:
The brow becalms us when 'tis smooth and plain,
And when 'tis wrinckled, shipwracks us again.
Smooth, 'tis a Paradice, where we would have
Immortal stay, and wrinkled 'tis our grave.
The Nose (like to the first Meridian) runs
Not 'twixt an East and West, but 'twixt two suns;
It leaves a Cheek, a rosie Hemisphere
On either side, and then directs us where
Upon the Islands fortunate we fall,
(Not faynte *Canaries,* but *Ambrosiall*)
Her swelling lips; To which when wee are come,
We anchor there, and think our selves at home,
For they seem all: there Syrens songs, and there
Wise Delphick Oracles do fill the ear;
There in a Creek where chosen pearls do swell,
The Remora, her cleaving tongue doth dwell.
These, and the glorious Promontory, her Chin
Ore past; and the streight *Hellespont* betweene
The *Sestos* and *Abydos* of her breasts,
(Not of two Lovers, but two Loves the neasts)
Succeeds a boundless sea, but yet thine eye
Some Island moles may scattered there descry;
And Sailing towards her *India,* in that way
Shall at her fair Atlantick Navell stay;
Though thence the Current be thy Pilot made,
Yet ere thou be where thou wouldst be embay'd,
Thou shalt upon another Forest set,

Where many Shipwrack, and no further get.
When thou art there, consider what this chace
Mispent by thy beginning at the face,
    Rather set out below; practice my Art,
Some Symetry the foot hath with that part
Which thou dost seek, and is thy Map for that
Lovely enough to stop, but not stay at:
Least subject to disguise and change it is;
Men say the Devil never can change his.
It is the Emblem that hath figured
Firmness; 'tis the first part that comes to bed.
Civilitie we see refin'd: the kiss
Which at the face began, transplanted is,
Since to the hand, since to the Imperial knee,
Now at the Papal foot delights to be:
If Kings think that the nearer way, and do
Rise from the foot, Lovers may do so too;
For as free Spheres move faster far then can
Birds, whom the air resists, so may that man
Which goes this empty and Ætherial way,
Then if at beauties elements he stay.
Rich Nature hath in women wisely made
Two purses, and their mouths aversely laid:
They then, which to the lower tribute owe,
That way which that Exchequer looks, must go:
He which doth not, his error is as great,
As who by Clyster gave the Stomack meat.

Loves Usury

For every houre that thou wilt spare mee now,
    I will allow,
Usurious God of Love, twenty to thee,
When with my browne, my gray haires equall bee;
Till then, Love, let my body raigne, and let
Mee travell, sojourne, snatch, plot, have, forget,
Resume my last yeares relict: thinke that yet
    We'had never met.

Let mee thinke any rivalls letter mine,
    And at next nine
Keepe midnights promise; mistake by the way
The maid, and tell the Lady of that delay;
Onely let mee love none, no, not the sport;
From country grasse, to comfitures of Court,
Or cities quelque choses, let report
    My minde transport.

This bargaine's good; if when I'am old, I bee
    Inflam'd by thee,
If thine owne honour, or my shame, or paine,
Thou covet most, at that age thou shalt gaine.
Doe thy will then, then subject and degree,
And fruit of love, Love I submit to thee,
Spare mee till then, I'll beare it, though she bee
    One that loves mee.

ELEGIE XX Loves Warre

Till I have peace with thee, warr other men,
And when I have peace, can I leave thee then?
All other Warrs are scrupulous; Only thou
O fayr free Citty, maist thyselfe allowe
To any one: In Flanders, who can tell
Whether the Master presse; or men rebell?
Only we know, that which all Ideots say,
They beare most blows which come to part the fray.
France in her lunatique giddiness did hate
Ever our men, yea and our God of late;
Yet she relyes upon our Angels well,
Which nere returne; no more then they which fell.
Sick Ireland is with a strange warr possest
Like to an Ague; now raging, now at rest;
Which time will cure: yet it must doe her good
If she were purg'd, and her head vayne let blood.
And Midas joyes our Spanish journeys give,
We touch all gold, but find no food to live.
And I should be in the hott parching clyme,
To dust and ashes turn'd before my time.
To mew me in a Ship, is to inthrall
Mee in a prison, that weare like to fall;
Or in a Cloyster; save that there men dwell
In a calme heaven, here in a swaggering hell.
Long voyages are long consumptions,
And ships are carts for executions.
Yea they are Deaths; Is't not all one to flye
Into an other World, as t'is to dye?
Here let mee warr; in these armes lett mee lye;
Here lett mee parlee, batter, bleede, and dye.
Thyne armes imprison me, and myne armes thee;
Thy hart thy ransome is; take myne for mee.
Other men war that they their rest may gayne;

But wee will rest that wee may fight agayne.
Those warrs the ignorant, these th'experienc'd love,
There wee are alwayes under, here above.
There Engins farr off breed a just true feare,
Neere thrusts, pikes, stabs, yea bullets hurt not here.
There lyes are wrongs; here safe uprightly lye;
There men kill men, we'will make one by and by.
Thou nothing; I not halfe so much shall do
In these Warrs, as they may which from us two
Shall spring. Thousands wee see which travaile not
To warrs; But stay swords, armes, and shott
To make at home; And shall not I do then
More glorious service, staying to make men?

The Message

Send home my long strayd eyes to mee,
Which (Oh) too long have dwelt on thee;
Yet since there they have learn'd such ill,
     Such forc'd fashions,
     And false passions,
          That they be
          Made by thee
Fit for no good sight, keep them still.

Send home my harmlesse heart againe,
Which no unworthy thought could staine;
But if it be taught by thine
     To make jestings
     Of protestings,
          And crosse both
          Word and oath,
Keepe it, for then 'tis none of mine.

Yet send me back my heart and eyes,
That I may know, and see thy lyes,
And may laugh and joy, when thou
     Art in anguish
     And dost languish
          For some one
          That will none,
Or prove as false as thou art now.

Natures lay Ideot, I taught thee to love,
And in that sophistrie, Oh, thou dost prove
Too subtile: Foole, thou didst not understand
The mystique language of the eye nor hand:
Nor couldst thou judge the difference of the aire
Of sighes, and say, this lies, this sounds despaire:
Nor by the'eyes water call a maladie
Desperately hot, or changing feaverously.
I had not taught thee then, the Alphabet
Of flowers, how they devisefully being set
And bound up, might with speechlesse secrecie
Deliver arrands mutely, and mutually.
Remember since all thy words us'd to bee
'To every suitor; *I, if my friends agree;*
Since, household charmes, thy husbands name to teach,
Were all the love trickes, that thy wit could reach;
And since, an houres discourse could scarce have made
One answer in thee, and that ill arraid
In broken proverbs, and torne sentences.
Thou art not by so many duties his,
That from the worlds Common having sever'd thee,
Inlaid thee, neither to be seene, nor see,
As mine: who have with amorous delicacies
Refin'd thee'into a blis-full Paradise.
Thy graces and good words my creatures bee;
I planted knowledge and lifes tree in thee,
Which Oh, shall strangers taste? Must I alas
Frame and enamell Plate, and drinke in Glasse?
Chafe waxe for others seales? breake a colts force
And leave him then, beeing made a ready horse?

Negative Love

I never stoop'd so low, as they
Which on an eye, cheeke, lip, can prey,
　　Seldome to them, which soare no higher
　　Then vertue or the minde to'admire,
For sense, and understanding may
　　Know, what gives fuell to their fire;
My love, though silly, is more brave,
For may I misse, when ere I crave,
If I know yet, what I would have.

If that be simply perfectest
Which can by no way be exprest
　　But *Negatives*, my love is so.
　　To All, which all love, I say no.
If any who deciphers best,
　　What we know not, our selves, can know,
Let him teach mee that nothing; This
As yet my ease, and comfort is,
Though I speed not, I cannot misse.

A Nocturnall upon S. Lucies Day
Being the shortest day

'Tis the yeares midnight, and it is the dayes,
Lucies, who scarce seaven houres herself unmaskes,
   The Sunne is spent, and now his flasks
   Send forth light squibs, no constant rayes;
     The worlds whole sap is sunke:
The generall balme th'hydroptique earth hath drunk,
Whither, as to the beds-feet, life is shrunke,
Dead and enterr'd; yet all these seeme to laugh,
Compar'd with mee, who am their Epitaph.

Study me then, you who shall lovers bee
At the next world, that is, at the next Spring:
   For I am every dead thing,
   In whom love wrought new Alchimie.
     For his art did expresse
A quintessence even from nothingnesse,
From dull privations, and leane emptinesse:
He ruin'd mee, and I am re-begot
Of absence, darknesse, death; things which are not.

All others, from all things, draw all that's good,
Life, soule, forme, spirit, whence they beeing have;
   I, by loves limbecke, am the grave
   Of all, that's nothing. Oft a flood
     Have wee two wept, and so
Drownd the whole world, us two; oft did we grow
To be two Chaosses, when we did show
Care to ought else; and often absences
Withdrew our soules, and made us carcasses.

But I am by her death, (which word wrongs her)
Of the first nothing, the Elixer grown;
   Were I a man, that I were one,
   I needs must know; I should preferre,
      If I were any beast,
Some ends, some means; Yea plants, yea stones detest,
And love; All, all some properties invest;
If I an ordinary nothing were,
As shadow, a light, and body must be here.

But I am None; nor will my Sunne renew.
You lovers, for whose sake, the lesser Sunne
   At this time to the Goat is runne
   To fetch new lust, and give it you,
      Enjoy your summer all;
Since shee enjoyes her long nights festivall,
Let mee prepare towards her, and let mee call
This houre her Vigill, and her Eve, since this
Both the yeares, and the dayes deep midnight is.

Oh, let mee not serve so, as those men serve
Whom honours smoakes at once fatten and sterve;
Poorely enrich't with great mens words or lookes;
Nor so write my name in thy loving bookes
As those Idolatrous flatterers, which still
Their Princes stiles, with many Realmes fulfill
Whence they no tribute have, and where no sway.
Such services I offer as shall pay
Themselves, I hate dead names: Oh then let mee
Favorite in Ordinary, or no favorite bee.
When my Soule was in her owne body sheath'd,
Nor yet by oathes betroth'd, nor kisses breath'd
Into my Purgatory, faithlesse thee,
Thy heart seem'd waxe, and Steele thy constancie:
So carelesse flowers strow'd on the waters face,
The curled whirlepooles suck, smack, and embrace,
Yet drowne them; so, the tapers beamie eye
Amorously twinkling, beckens the giddie flie,
Yet burnes his wings; and such the devill is,
Scarce visiting them, who are intirely his.
When I behold a streame, which, from the spring,
Doth with doubtfull melodious murmuring,
Or in a speechlesse slumber, calmely ride
Her wedded channels bosome, and then chide
And bend her browes, and swell if any bough
Do but stoop downe, or kisse her upmost brow;
Yet, if her often gnawing kisses winne
The traiterous banke to gape, and let her in,
She rusheth violently, and doth divorce
Her from her native, and her long-kept course,
And rores, and braves it, and in gallant scorne,
In flattering eddies promising retorne,
She flouts the channell, who thenceforth is drie;

Then say I; that is shee, and this am I.
Yet let not thy deepe bitternesse beget
Carelesse despaire in mee, for that will whet
My minde to scorne; and Oh, love dull'd with paine
Was ne'r so wise, nor well arm'd as disdaine.
Then with new eyes I shall survay thee,'and spie
Death in thy cheekes, and darknesse in thine eye.
Though hope bred faith and love; thus taught, I shall
As nations do from Rome, from thy love fall.
My hate shall outgrow thine, and utterly
I will renounce thy dalliance: and when I
Am the Recusant, in that resolute state,
What hurts it mee to be'excommunicate?

ELEGIE XVI On his Mistris

By our first strange and fatall interview,
By all desires which thereof did ensue,
By our long starving hopes, by that remorse
Which my words masculine perswasive force
Begot in thee, and by the memory
Of hurts, which spies and rivals threatned me,
I calmly beg: But by thy fathers wrath,
By all paines, which want and divorcement hath,
I conjure thee, and all the oathes which I
And thou have sworne to seale joynt constancy,
Here I unsweare, and overswear them thus,
Thou shalt not love by wayes so dangerous.
Temper, ô faire Love, loves impetuous rage,
Be my true Mistris still, not my faign'd Page;
I'll goe, and, by thy kinde leave, leave behinde
Thee, onely worthy to nurse in my minde,
Thirst to come backe; ô if thou die before,
My soule from other lands to thee shall soare.
Thy (else Almighty) beautie cannot move
Rage from the Seas, nor thy love teach them love,
Nor tame wilde Boreas harshnesse; Thou hast reade
How roughly hee in peeces shivered
Faire Orithea, whom he swore he lov'd.
Fall ill or good, 'tis madnesse to have prov'd
Dangers unurg'd; Feed on this flattery,
That absent Lovers one in th'other be.
Dissemble nothing, not a boy, nor change
Thy bodies habite, nor mindes; bee not strange
To thy selfe onely; All will spie in thy face
A blushing womanly discovering grace;
Richly cloath'd Apes, are call'd Apes, and as soone
Ecclips'd as bright we call the Moone the Moone.
Men of France, changeable Camelions,

Spittles of diseases, shops of fashions,
Loves fuellers, and the rightest company
Of Players, which upon the worlds stage be,
Will quickly know thee, and no lesse, alas!
Th'indifferent Italian, as we passe
His warme land, well content to thinke thee Page,
Will hunt thee with such lust, and hideous rage,
As *Lots* faire guests were vext. But none of these
Nor spungy hydroptique Dutch shall thee displease,
If thou stay here. O stay here, for, for thee
England is onely a worthy Gallerie,
To walke in expectation, till from thence
Our greatest King call thee to his presence.
When I am gone, dreame me some happinesse,
Nor let thy lookes our long hid love confesse,
Nor praise, nor dispraise me, nor blesse nor curse
Openly loves force, nor in bed fright thy Nurse
With midnights startings, crying out, oh, oh
Nurse, ô my love is slaine, I saw him goe
O'r the white Alpes alone; I saw him I,
Assail'd, fight, taken, stabb'd, bleed, fall, and die.
Augure me better chance, except dread *Jove*
Thinke it enough for me to'have had thy love.

The Paradox

No Lover saith, I love, nor any other
    Can judge a perfect Lover;
Hee thinkes that else none can, nor will agree
    That any loves but hee:
I cannot say I lov'd, for who can say
    Hee was kill'd yesterday?
Love with excesse of heat, more yong then old,
    Death kills with too much cold;
Wee dye but once, and who lov'd last did die,
    Hee that saith twice, doth lye:
For though hee seeme to move, and stirre a while,
    It doth the sense beguile.
Such life is like the light which bideth yet
    When the lights life is set,
Or like the heat, which fire in solid matter
    Leaves behinde, two houres after.
Once I lov'd and dy'd; and am now become
    Mine Epitaph and Tombe.
Here dead men speake their last, and so do I;
    Love-slaine, loe, here I lye.

ELEGIE VI The Perfume

Once, and but once found in thy company,
All thy suppos'd escapes are laid on mee;
And as a thiefe at barre, is question'd there
By all the men, that have beene rob'd that yeare,
So am I, (by this traiterous meanes surpriz'd)
By thy Hydroptique father catechiz'd.
Though he had wont to search with glazed eyes,
As though he came to kill a Cockatrice,
Though hee hath oft sworne, that hee would remove
Thy beauties beautie, and food of our love,
Hope of his goods, if I with thee were seene,
Yet close and secret, as our soules, we'have beene.
Though thy immortall mother which doth lye
Still buried in her bed, yet will not dye,
Takes this advantage to sleepe out day-light,
And watch thy entries, and returnes all night,
And, when she takes thy hand, and would seeme kind,
Doth search what rings, and armelets she can finde,
And kissing notes the colour of thy face,
And fearing least thou'art swolne, doth thee embrace;
To trie if thou long, doth name strange meates,
And notes thy palenesse, blushing, sighs, and sweats;
And politiquely will to thee confesse
The sinnes of her owne youths ranke lustinesse;
Yet love these Sorceries did remove, and move
Thee to gull thine owne mother for my love.
Thy little brethren, which like Faiery Sprights
Oft skipt into our chamber, those sweet nights,
And kist, and ingled on thy fathers knee,
Were brib'd next day, to tell what they did see:
The grim eight-foot-high iron-bound serving-man,
That oft names God in oathes, and onely than,
He that to barre the first gate, doth as wide

As the great Rhodian Colossus stride,
Which, if in hell no other paines there were,
Makes mee feare hell, because he must be there:
Though by thy father he were hir'd to this,
Could never witnesse any touch or kisse.
But Oh, too common ill, I brought with mee
That, which betray'd mee to my enemie:
A loud perfume, which at my entrance cryed
Even at thy fathers nose, so were wee spied.
When, like a tyran King, that in his bed
Smelt gunpowder, the pale wretch shivered.
Had it beene some bad smell, he would have thought
That his owne feet, or breath, that smell had wrought.
But as wee in our Ile emprisoned,
Where cattell onely, 'and diverse dogs are bred,
The pretious Vnicornes, strange monsters call,
So thought he good, strange, that had none at all.
I taught my silkes, their whistling to forbeare,
Even my opprest shoes, dumbe and speechlesse were,
Onely, thou bitter sweet, whom I had laid
Next mee, mee traiterously hast betraid,
And unsuspected hast invisibly
At once fled unto him, and staid with mee.
Base excrement of earth, which dost confound
Sense, from distinguishing the sicke from sound;
By thee the seely Amorous sucks his death
By drawing in a leprous harlots breath;
By thee, the greatest staine to mans estate
Falls on us, to be call'd effeminate;
Though you be much lov'd in the Princes hall,
There, things that seeme, exceed substantiall;
Gods, when yee fum'd on altars, were pleas'd well,
Because you'were burnt, not that they lik'd your smell;
You'are loathsome all, being taken simply alone,
Shall wee love ill things joyn'd, and hate each one?
If you were good, your good doth soone decay;

And you are rare, that takes the good away.
All my perfumes, I give most willingly
To'embalme thy fathers corse; What? will hee die?

The Primrose

*being at Mountgomery Castle, upon the hill, on which
it is situate*

Upon this Primrose hill,
     Where, if Heav'n would distill
A shoure of raine, each severall drop might goe
To his owne primrose, and grow Manna so;
And where their forme, and their infinitie
     Make a terrestriall Galaxie,
     As the small starres doe in the skie:
I walke to finde a true Love; and I see
That 'tis not a mere woman, that is shee,
But must, or more, or lesse then woman bee.

Yet know I not, which flower
     I wish; a sixe, or foure;
For should my true-Love lesse then woman bee,
She were scarce any thing; and then, should she
Be more then woman, shee would get above
     All thought of sexe, and thinke to move
     My heart to study her, and not to love;
Both these were monsters; Since there must reside
Falshood in woman, I could more abide,
She were by art, then Nature falsify'd.

Live Primrose then, and thrive
     With thy true number five;
And women, whom this flower doth represent,
With this mysterious number be content;
Ten is the farthest number; if halfe ten
     Belonge unto each woman, then
     Each woman may take halfe us men;
Or if this will not serve their turne, Since all
Numbers are odde, or even, and they fall
First into this, five, women may take us all.

Of the Progress of the Soule

The Second Anniversarie

Nothing could make me sooner to confesse
That this world had an everlastingnesse,
Then to consider, that a yeare is runne,
Since both this lower world's, and the Sunnes Sunne,
The Lustre, and the vigor of this All,
Did set; 'twere blasphemie to say, did fall.
But as a ship which hath strooke saile, doth runne
By force of that force which before, it wonne:
Or as sometimes in a beheaded man,
Though at those two Red seas, which freely ranne,
One from the Trunke, another from the Head,
His soule be sail'd, to her eternall bed,
His eyes will twinckle, and his tongue will roll,
As though he beckned, and cal'd backe his soule,
He graspes his hands, and he pulls up his feet,
And seemes to reach, and to step forth to meet
His soule; when all these motions which we saw,
Are but as Ice, which crackles at a thaw:
Or as a Lute, which in moist weather, rings
Her knell alone, by cracking of her strings:
So struggles this dead world, now shee is gone;
For there is motion in corruption.
As some daies are at the Creation nam'd,
Before the Sunne, the which fram'd daies, was fram'd,
So after this Sunne's set, some shew appeares,
And orderly vicissitude of yeares.
Yet a new Deluge, and of *Lethe* flood,
Hath drown'd us all, All have forgot all good,
Forgetting her, the maine reserve of all.
Yet in this deluge, grosse and generall,
Thou seest me strive for life; my life shall bee,
To be hereafter prais'd, for praysing thee;

Immortall Maid, who though thou would'st refuse
The name of Mother, be unto my Muse
A Father, since her chast Ambition is,
Yearely to bring forth such a child as this.
These Hymnes may worke on future wits, and so
May great Grand children of thy prayses grow.
And so, though not revive, embalme and spice
The world, which else would putrifie with vice.
For thus, Man may extend thy progeny,
Until man doe but vanish, and not die.
These Hymnes thy issue, may encrease so long,
As till Gods great *Venite* change the song.
Thirst for that time, O my insatiate soule,
And serve thy thirst, with Gods safe-sealing Bowle.
Be thirstie still, and drinke still till thou goe
To th'only Health, to be Hydroptique so.
Forget this rotten world; And unto thee
Let thine owne times as an old storie bee.
Be not concern'd: studie not why, nor when;
Doe not so much as not beleeve a man.
For though to erre, be worst, to try truths forth,
Is far more businesse, then this world is worth.
The world is but a carkasse; thou art fed
By it, but as a worme, that carkasse bred;
And why should'st thou, poore worme, consider more,
When this world will grow better then before,
Then those thy fellow wormes doe thinke upon
That carkasses last resurrection.
Forget this world, and scarce thinke of it so,
As of old clothes, cast off a yeare agoe.
To be thus stupid is Alacritie;
Men thus Lethargique have best Memory.
Look upward; that's towards her, whose happy state
We now lament not, but congratulate.
Shee, to whom all this world was but a stage,
Where all sat harkning how her youthfull age

Should be emploi'd, because in all shee did,
Some Figure of the Golden times was hid.
Who could not lacke, what e'r this world could give,
Because shee was the forme, that made it live;
Nor could complaine, that this world was unfit
To be staid in, then when shee was in it;
Shee that first tried indifferent desires
By vertue, and vertue by religious fires,
Shee to whose person Paradise adher'd,
As Courts to Princes, shee whose eyes ensphear'd
Star-light enough, t'have made the South controule,
(Had shee beene there) the Star-full Northerne Pole,
Shee, shee is gone; she is gone; when thou knowest this,
What fragmentary rubbidge this world is
Thou knowest, and that it is not worth a thought;
He honors it too much that thinkes it nought.
Thinke then, my soule, that death is but a Groome,
Which brings a Taper to the outward roome,
Whence thou spiest first a little glimmering light,
And after brings it nearer to thy sight:
For such approaches doth heaven make in death.
Thinke thy selfe labouring now with broken breath,
And thinke those broken and soft Notes to bee
Division, and thy happyest Harmonie.
Thinke thee laid on thy death-bed, loose and slacke;
And thinke that, but unbinding of a packe,
To take one precious thing, thy soule from thence.
Thinke thy selfe parch'd with fevers violence,
Anger thine ague more, by calling it
Thy Physicke; chide the slacknesse of the fit.
Thinke that thou hear'st thy knell, and think no more,
But that, as Bels cal'd thee to Church before,
So this, to the Triumphant Church, calls thee.
Thinke Satans Sergeants round about thee bee,
And thinke that but for Legacies they thrust;
Give one thy Pride, to'another give thy Lust:

Give them those sinnes which they gave thee before,
And trust th'immaculate blood to wash thy score.
Thinke thy friends weeping round, and thinke that they
Weepe but because they goe not yet thy way.
Thinke that they close thine eyes, and thinke in this,
That they confesse much in the world, amisse,
Who dare not trust a dead mans eye with that,
Which they from God, and Angels cover not.
Thinke that they shroud thee up, and think from thence
They reinvest thee in white innocence.
Thinke that thy body rots, and (if so low,
Thy soule exalted so, thy thoughts can goe,)
Think thee a Prince, who of themselves create
Wormes which insensibly devoure their State.
Thinke that they bury thee, and thinke that right
Laies thee to sleepe but a Saint Lucies night.
Thinke these things cheerefully: and if thou bee
Drowsie or slacke, remember then that shee,
Shee whose Complexion was so even made,
That which of her Ingredients should invade
The other three, no Feare, no Art could guesse:
So far were all remov'd from more or lesse.
But as in Mithridate, or just perfumes,
Where all good things being met, no one presumes
To governe, or to triumph on the rest,
Only because all were, no part was best.
And as, though all doe know, that quantities
Are made of lines, and lines from Points arise,
None can these lines or quantities unjoynt,
And say this is a line, or this a point,
So though the Elements and Humors were
In her, one could not say, this governes there.
Whose even constitution might have wonne
Any disease to venter on the Sunne,
Rather then her: and make a spirit feare,
That hee to disuniting subject were.

To whose proportions if we would compare
Cubes, th'are unstable; Circles, Angular;
She who was such a chaine as Fate employes
To bring mankinde all Fortunes it enjoyes;
So fast, so even wrought, as one would thinke,
No Accident could threaten any linke;
Shee, shee embrac'd a sicknesse, gave it meat,
The purest blood, and breath, that e'r it eate;
And hath taught us, that though a good man hath
Title to heaven, and plead it by his Faith,
And though he may pretend a conquest, since
Heaven was content to suffer violence,
Yea though hee plead a long possession too,
(For they're in heaven on earth who heavens workes do)
Though hee had right and power and place, before,
Yet Death must usher, and unlocke the doore.
Thinke further on thy selfe, my Soule, and thinke
How thou at first wast made but in a sinke;
Thinke that it argued some infirmitie,
That those two soules, which then thou foundst in me,
Thou fedst upon, and drewst into thee, both
My second soule of sense, and first of growth.
Thinke but how poore thou wast, how obnoxious;
Whom a small lumpe of flesh could poyson thus.
This curded milke, this poore unlittered whelpe
My body, could, beyond escape or helpe,
Infect thee with Originall sinne, and thou
Couldst neither then refuse, nor leave it now.
Thinke that no stubborne sullen Anchorit,
Which fixt to a pillar, or a grave, doth sit
Bedded, and bath'd in all his ordures, dwels
So fowly as our Soules in their first-built Cels.
Thinke in how poore a prison thou didst lie
After, enabled but to suck, and crie.
Thinke, when'twas growne to most,'twas a poore Inne,
A Province pack'd up in two yards of skinne,

And that usurp'd or threatned with the rage
Of sicknesses, or their true mother, Age.
But thinke that Death hath now enfranchise'd thee,
Thou hast thy'expansion now, and libertie;
Thinke that a rustie Peece, discharg'd, is flowne
In peeces, and the bullet is his owne,
And freely flies: This to thy Soule allow,
Thinke thy shell broke, thinke thy Soule hatch'd but now.
And think this slow-pac'd soule, which late did cleave
To'a body, and went but by the bodies leave,
Twenty, perchance, or thirty mile a day,
Dispatches in a minute all the way
Twixt heaven, and earth; she stayes not in the ayre,
To looke what Meteors there themselves prepare;
She carries no desire to know, nor sense,
Whether th'ayres middle region be intense;
For th'Element of fire, she doth not know,
Whether she past by such a place or no;
She baits not at the Moone, nor cares to trie
Whether in that new world, men live, and die.
Venus retards her not, to'enquire, how shee
Can, (being one starre) *Hesper,* and *Vesper* bee;
Hee that charm'd *Argus* eyes, sweet *Mercury,*
Workes not on her, who now is growne all eye;
Who, if she meet the body of the Sunne,
Goes through, not staying till his course be runne;
Who findes in *Mars* his Campe no corps of Guard;
Nor is by *Jove,* nor by his father barr'd;
But ere she can consider how she went,
At once is at, and through the Firmament.
And as these starres were but so many beads
Strung on one string, speed undistinguish'd leads
Her through those Spheares, as through the beads, a string,
Whose quick succession makes it still one thing:
As doth the pith, which, lest our bodies slacke,
Strings fast the little bones of necke, and backe;

So by the Soule doth death string Heaven and Earth;
For when our Soule enjoyes this her third birth,
(Creation gave her one, a second, grace,)
Heaven is as neare, and present to her face,
As colours are, and objects, in a roome
Where darknesse was before, when Tapers come.
This must, my Soule, thy long-short Progresse bee;
To'advance these thoughts, remember then, that shee,
Shee, whose faire body no such prison was,
But that a Soule might well be pleas'd to passe
An age in her; she whose rich beauty lent
Mintage to other beauties, for they went
But for so much as they were like to her;
Shee, in whose body (if we dare preferre
This low world, to so high a marke as shee,)
The Westerne treasure, Easterne spicerie,
Europe, and Afrique, and the unknowne rest
Were easily found, or what in them was best;
And when w'have made this large discoverie
Of all, in her some one part then will bee
Twenty such parts, whose plenty and riches is
Enough to make twenty such worlds as this;
Shee, whom had they knowne who did first betroth
The Tutelar Angels, and assign'd one, both
To Nations, Cities, and to Companies,
To Functions, Offices, and Dignities,
And to each severall man, to him, and him,
They would have given her one for every limbe;
She, of whose soule, if wee may say, 'twas Gold,
Her body was th'Electrum, and did hold
Many degrees of that; wee understood
Her by her sight; her pure, and eloquent blood
Spoke in her cheekes, and so distinctly wrought,
That one might almost say, her body thought;
Shee, shee, thus richly and largely hous'd, is gone:
And chides us slow-pac'd snailes who crawle upon

Our prisons prison, earth, nor thinke us well,
Longer, then whil'st wee beare our brittle shell.
But 'twere but little to have chang'd our roome,
If, as we were in this our living Tombe
Oppress'd with ignorance, wee still were so.
Poore soule, in this thy flesh what dost thou know?
Thou know'st thy selfe so little, as thou know'st not,
How thou didst die, nor how thou wast begot.
Thou neither know'st, how thou at first cam'st in,
Nor how thou took'st the poyson of mans sinne.
Nor dost thou, (though thou know'st, that thou art so)
By what way thou art made immortall, know.
Thou art too narrow, wretch, to comprehend
Even thy selfe: yea though thou wouldst but bend
To know thy body. Have not all soules thought
For many ages, that our body'is wrought
Of Ayre, and Fire, and other Elements?
And now they thinke of new ingredients,
And one Soule thinkes one, and another way
Another thinkes, and 'tis an even lay.
Knowst thou but how the stone doth enter in
The bladders cave, and never breake the skinne?
Know'st thou how blood, which to the heart doth flow,
Doth from one ventricle to th'other goe?
And for the putrid stuffe, which thou dost spit,
Know'st thou how thy lungs have attracted it?
There are no passages, so that there is
(For ought thou know'st) piercing of substances.
And of those many opinions which men raise
Of Nailes and Haires, dost thou know which to praise?
What hope have wee to know our selves, when wee
Know not the least things, which for our use be?
Wee see in Authors, too stiffe to recant,
A hundred controversies of an Ant;
And yet one watches, starves, freeses, and sweats,
To know but Catechismes and Alphabets

Of unconcerning things, matters of fact;
How others on our stage their parts did Act;
What *Cæsar* did, yea, and what *Cicero* said.
Why grasse is greene, or why our blood is red,
Are mysteries which none have reach'd unto.
In this low forme, poore soule, what wilt thou doe?
When wilt thou shake off this Pedantery,
Of being taught by sense, and Fantasie?
Thou look'st through spectacles; small things seeme great
Below; But up unto the watch-towre get,
And see all things despoyl'd of fallacies:
Thou shalt not peepe through lattices of eyes,
Nor heare through Labyrinths of eares, nor learne
By circuit, or collections to discerne.
In heaven thou straight know'st all, concerning it,
And what concernes it not, shalt straight forget.
There thou (but in no other schoole) maist bee
Perchance, as learned, and as full, as shee,
Shee who all libraries had throughly read
At home in her owne thoughts, and practised
So much good as would make as many more:
Shee whose example they must all implore,
Who would or doe, or thinke well, and confesse
That all the vertuous Actions they expresse,
Are but a new, and worse edition
Of her some one thought, or one action:
She who in th'art of knowing Heaven, was growne
Here upon earth, to such perfection,
That she hath, ever since to Heaven she came,
(In a far fairer print,) but read the same:
Shee, shee not satisfied with all this waight,
(For so much knowledge, as would over-fraight
Another, did but ballast her) is gone
As well t'enjoy, as get perfection.
And cals us after her, in that shee tooke,
(Taking her selfe) our best, and worthiest booke.

Returne not, my Soule, from this extasie,
And meditation of what thou shalt bee,
To earthly thoughts, till it to thee appeare,
With whom thy conversation must be there.
With whom wilt thou converse? what station
Canst thou choose out, free from infection,
That will not give thee theirs, nor drinke in thine?
Shalt thou not finde a spungie slacke Divine
Drinke and sucke in th'instructions of Great men,
And for the word of God, vent them agen?
Are there not some Courts (and then, no things bee
So like as Courts) which, in this let us see,
That wits and tongues of Libellers are weake,
Because they do more ill, then these can speake?
The poyson's gone through all, poysons affect
Chiefly the chiefest parts, but some effect
In nailes, and haires, yea excrements, will show;
So lyes the poyson of sinne in the most low.
Up, up, my drowsie Soule, where thy new eare
Shall in the Angels songs no discord heare;
Where thou shalt see the blessed Mother-maid
Joy in not being that, which men have said.
Where she is exalted more for being good,
Then for her interest of Mother-hood.
Up to those Patriarchs, which did longer sit
Expecting Christ, then they'have enjoy'd him yet.
Up to those Prophets, which now gladly see
Their Prophesies growne to be Historie.
Up to th'Apostles, who did bravely runne
All the Suns course, with more light then the Sunne.
Up to those Martyrs, who did calmly bleed
Oyle to th'Apostles Lamps, dew to their seed.
Up to those Virgins, who thought, that almost
They made joyntenants with the Holy Ghost,
If they to any should his Temple give.
Up, up, for in that squadron there doth live

She, who hath carried thither new degrees
(As to their number) to their dignities.
Shee, who being to her selfe a State, injoy'd
All royalties which any State employ'd;
For shee made warres, and triumph'd; reason still
Did not o'rthrow, but rectifie her will:
And she made peace, for no peace is like this,
That beauty, and chastity together kisse:
She did high justice, for she crucified
Every first motion of rebellious pride:
And she gave pardons, and was liberall,
For, onely her selfe except, she pardon'd all:
Shee coy'nd, in this, that her impressions gave
To all our actions all the worth they have:
She gave protections; the thoughts of her brest
Satans rude Officers could ne'r arrest.
As these prerogatives being met in one,
Made her a soveraigne State; religion
Made her a Church; and these two made her all.
She who was all this All, and could not fall
To worse, by company, (for she was still
More Antidote, then all the world was ill,)
Shee, shee doth leave it, and by Death, survive
All this, in Heaven; whither who doth not strive
The more, because shees there, he doth not know
That accidentall joyes in Heaven doe grow.
But pause, my soule; And study, ere thou fall
On accidentall joyes, th'essentiall.
Still before Accessories doe abide
A triall, must the principall be tride.
And what essentiall joy can'st thou expect
Here upon earth? what permanent effect
Of transitory causes? Dost thou love
Beauty? (And beauty worthy'st is to move)
Poore cousened cousenor, *that* she, and *that* thou,
Which did begin to love, are neither now;

You are both fluid, chang'd since yesterday;
Next day repaires, (but ill) last dayes decay.
Nor are, (although the river keepe the name)
Yesterdaies waters, and to daies the same.
So flowes her face, and thine eyes, neither now
That Saint, nor Pilgrime, which your loving vow
Concern'd, remaines; but whil'st you thinke you bee
Constant, you'are hourely in inconstancie.
Honour may have pretence unto our love,
Because that God did live so long above
Without this Honour, and then lov'd it so,
That he at last made Creatures to bestow
Honour on him; not that he needed it,
But that, to his hands, man might grow more fit.
But since all Honours from inferiours flow,
(For they doe give it; Princes doe but shew
Whom they would have so honor'd) and that this
On such opinions, and capacities
Is built, as rise and fall, to more and lesse:
Alas, 'tis but a casuall happinesse.
Hath ever any man to'himselfe assign'd
This or that happinesse to'arrest his minde,
But that another man which takes a worse,
Thinks him a foole for having tane that course?
They who did labour Babels tower to'erect,
Might have considered, that for that effect,
All this whole solid Earth could not allow
Nor furnish forth materialls enow;
And that this Center, to raise such a place,
Was farre too little, to have beene the Base;
No more affords this world, foundation
To erect true joy, were all the meanes in one.
But as the Heathen made them severall gods,
Of all Gods Benefits, and all his Rods,
(For as the Wine, and Corne, and Onions are
Gods unto them, so Agues bee, and Warre)

And as by changing that whole precious Gold
To such small Copper coynes, they lost the old,
And lost their only God, who ever must
Be sought alone, and not in such a thrust:
So much mankinde true happinesse mistakes;
No Joy enjoyes that man, that many makes.
Then, Soule, to thy first pitch worke up againe;
Know that all lines which circles doe containe,
For once that they the Center touch, doe touch
Twice the circumference; and be thou such;
Double on heaven thy thoughts on earth emploid;
All will not serve; Only who have enjoy'd
The sight of God, in fulnesse, can thinke it;
For it is both the object, and the wit.
This is essentiall joy, where neither hee
Can suffer diminution, nor wee;
'Tis such a full, and such a filling good,
Had th'Angels once look'd on him, they had stood.
To fill the place of one of them, or more,
Shee whom wee celebrate, is gone before.
She, who had Here so much essentiall joy,
As no chance could distract, much lesse destroy;
Who with Gods presence was acquainted so,
(Hearing, and speaking to him) as to know
His face in any naturall Stone, or Tree,
Better then when in Images they bee:
Who kept by diligent devotion,
Gods Image, in such reparation,
Within her heart, that what decay was growne,
Was her first Parents fault, and not her owne:
Who being solicited to any act,
Still heard God pleading his safe precontract;
Who by a faithfull confidence, was here
Betroth'd to God, and now is married there;
Whose twilights were more cleare, then our mid-day;
Who dreamt devoutlier, then most use to pray;

Who being here fil'd with grace, yet strove to bee,
Both where more grace, and more capacitie
At once is given: she to Heaven is gone,
Who made this world in some proportion
A heaven, and here, became unto us all,
Joy, (as our joyes admit) essentiall.
But could this low world joyes essentiall touch,
Heavens accidentall joyes would passe them much.
How poore and lame, must then our casuall bee?
If thy Prince will his subjects to call thee
My Lord, and this doe swell thee, thou art than,
By being greater, growne to bee lesse Man.
When no Physitian of redresse can speake,
A joyfull casuall violence may breake
A dangerous Apostem in thy breast;
And whil'st thou joyest in this, the dangerous rest,
The bag may rise up, and so strangle thee.
What e'r was casuall, may ever bee.
What should the nature change? Or make the same
Certaine, which was but casuall, when it came?
All casuall joy doth loud and plainly say,
Only by comming, that it can away.
Only in Heaven joyes strength is never spent;
And accidentall things are permanent.
Joy of a soules arrivall ne'r decaies;
For that soule ever joyes and ever staies.
Joy that their last great Consummation
Approaches in the resurrection;
When earthly bodies more celestiall
Shall be, then Angels were, for they could fall;
This kinde of joy doth every day admit
Degrees of growth, but none of losing it.
In this fresh joy, 'tis no small part, that shee,
Shee, in whose goodnesse, he that names degree,
Doth injure her; ('Tis losse to be cal'd best,
There where the stuffe is not such as the rest)

Shee, who left such a bodie, as even shee
Only in Heaven could learne, how it can bee
Made better; for shee rather was two soules,
Or like to full on both sides written Rols,
Where eyes might reade upon the outward skin,
As strong Records for God, as mindes within;
Shee, who by making full perfection grow,
Peeces a Circle, and still keepes it so,
Long'd for, and longing for it, to heaven is gone,
Where shee receives, and gives addition.
Here in a place, where mis-devotion frames
A thousand Prayers to Saints, whose very names
The ancient Church knew not, Heaven knows not yet:
And where, what lawes of Poetry admit,
Lawes of Religion have at least the same,
Immortall Maide, I might invoke thy name.
Could any Saint provoke that appetite,
Thou here should'st make me a French convertite.
But thou would'st not; nor would'st thou be content,
To take this, for my second yeares true Rent,
Did this Coine beare any other stampe, then his,
That gave thee power to doe, me, to say this.
Since his will is, that to posteritie,
Thou should'st for life, and death, a patterne bee,
And that the world should notice have of this,
The purpose, and th'Authoritie is his;
Thou art the Proclamation; and I am
The Trumpet, at whose voyce the people came.

The Prohibition

Take heed of loving mee,
At least remember, I forbade it thee;
Not that I shall repaire my'unthrifty wast
Of Breath and Blood, upon thy sighes, and teares,
By being to thee then what to me thou wast;
But, so great Joy, our life at once outweares,
Then, least thy love, by my death, frustrate bee,
If thou love mee, take heed of loving mee.

Take heed of hating mee,
Or too much triumph in the Victorie.
Not that I shall be mine owne officer,
And hate with hate againe retaliate;
But thou wilt lose the stile of conquerour,
If I, thy conquest, perish by thy hate.
Then, least my being nothing lessen thee,
If thou hate mee, take heed of hating mee.

Yet, love and hate mee too,
So, these extreames shall neithers office doe;
Love mee, that I may die the gentler way;
Hate mee, because thy love'is too great for mee;
Or let these two, themselves, not me decay;
So shall I, live, thy Stage, not triumph bee;
Lest thou thy love and hate and mee undoe,
To let mee live, O love and hate mee too.

The Relique

When my grave is broke up againe
Some second ghest to entertaine,
(For graves have learn'd that woman-head
To be to more then one a Bed)
    And he that digs it, spies
A bracelet of bright haire about the bone,
    Will he not let'us alone,
And thinke that there a loving couple lies,
Who thought that this device might be some way
To make their soules, at the last busie day,
Meet at this grave, and make a little stay?

If this fall in a time, or land,
Where mis-devotion doth command,
Then, he that digges us up, will bring
Us, to the Bishop, and the King,
    To make us Reliques; then
Thou shalt be a Mary Magdalen, and I
    A something else thereby;
All women shall adore us, and some men;
And since at such time, miracles are sought,
I would have that age by this paper taught
What miracles wee harmelesse lovers wrought.

First, we lov'd well and faithfully,
Yet knew not what wee lov'd, nor why,
Difference of sex no more wee knew,
Then our Guardian Angells doe;
    Comming and going, wee
Perchance might kisse, but not between those meales;
    Our hands ne'r toucht the seales,
Which nature, injur'd by late law, sets free:
These miracles wee did; but now alas,
All measure, and all language, I should passe,
Should I tell what a miracle shee was.

Show me deare Christ, thy spouse, so bright and clear,
What! is it She, which on the other shore
Goes richly painted? or which rob'd and tore
Laments and mournes in Germany and here?
Sleepes she a thousand, then peepes up one yeare?
Is she selfe truth and errs? now new, now outwore?
Doth she, and did she, and shall she evermore
On one, on seaven, or on no hill appeare?
Dwells she with us, or like adventuring knights
First travaile we to seeke and then make Love?
Betray kind husband thy spouse to our sights,
And let myne amorous soule court thy mild Dove,
Who is most trew, and pleasing to thee, then
When she'is embrac'd and open to most men.

The Sunne Rising

Busie old foole, unruly Sunne,
        Why dost thou thus,
Through windowes, and through curtaines call on us?
Must to thy motions lovers seasons run?
        Sawcy pedantique wretch, goe chide
        Late schoole boyes, and sowre prentices,
    Goe tell Court-huntsmen, that the King will ride,
    Call countrey ants to harvest offices;
Love, all alike, no season knowes, nor clyme,
Nor houres, dayes, moneths, which are the rags of time.

        Thy beames, so reverend, and strong
        Why shouldst thou thinke?
I could eclipse and cloud them with a winke,
But that I would not lose her sight so long:
        If her eyes have not blinded thine,
        Looke, and to morrow late, tell mee,
    Whether both the'India's of spice and Myne
    Be where thou leftst them, or lie here with mee.
Aske for those Kings whom thou saw'st yesterday,
And thou shalt heare, All here in one bed lay.

        She'is all States, and all Princes, I,
        Nothing else is.
Princes doe but play us; compar'd to this,
All honor's mimique; All wealth alchimie.
        Thou sunne art halfe as happy'as wee,
        In that the world's contracted thus;
    Thine age askes ease, and since thy duties bee
    To warme the world, that's done in warming us.
Shine here to us, and thou art every where;
This bed thy center is, these walls, thy spheare.

Song

Sweetest love, I do not goe,
   For wearinesse of thee,
Nor in hope the world can show
   A fitter Love for mee;
     But since that I
Must dye at last, 'tis best,
To use my selfe in jest
   Thus by fain'd deaths to dye;

Yesternight the Sunne went hence,
   And yet is here to day,
He hath no desire nor sense,
   Nor halfe so short a way:
     Then feare not mee,
But beleeve that I shall make
Speedier journeyes, since I take
   More wings and spurres then hee.

O how feeble is mans power,
   That if good fortune fall,
Cannot adde another houre,
   Nor a lost houre recall!
     But come bad chance,
And wee joyne to'it our strength,
And wee teach it art and length,
   It selfe o'r us to'advance.

When thou sigh'st, thou sigh'st not winde,
   But sigh'st my soule away,
When thou weep'st, unkindly kinde,
   My lifes blood doth decay.
     It cannot bee
That thou lov'st mee, as thou say'st,
If in thine my life thou waste,
   Thou art the best of mee.

Let not thy divining heart
    Forethinke me any ill,
Destiny may take thy part,
    And may thy feares fulfill
      But thinke that wee
Are but turn'd aside to sleepe;
They who one another keepe
    Alive, ne'r parted bee.

To a Jeat Ring sent to me

Thou art not so black, as my heart,
   Nor halfe so brittle, as her heart, thou art;
What would'st thou say? shall both our properties by thee bee spoke,
   Nothing more endlesse, nothing sooner broke?

Marriage rings are not of this stuffe;
   Oh, why should ought lesse precious, or lesse tough
Figure our loves? Except in thy name thou have bid it say,
   I'am cheap, and nought but fashion, fling me'away.

Yet stay with mee since thou art come,
   Circle this fingers top, which did'st her thombe.
Be justly proud, and gladly safe, that thou dost dwell with me,
   She that, Oh, broke her faith, would soon breake thee.

ELEGIE XIX To His Mistris, Going to bed

Come, Madam, come, all rest my powers defie,
Until I labour, I in labour lie.
The foe oft-times having the foe in sight,
Is tir'd with standing though he never fight.
Off with that girdle, like heavens Zone glittering,
But a far fairer world incompassing.
Unpin that spangled breastplate which you wear,
That th'eyes of busie fooles may be stopt there.
Unlace your self, for that harmonious chyme,
Tells me from you, that now it is bed time.
Off with that happy busk, which I envie,
That still can be, and still can stand so nigh.
Your gown going off, such beautious state reveals,
As when from flowry meads th'hills shadow steales.
Off with that wyerie Coronet and shew
The haiery Diademe which on you doth grow:
Now off with those shooes, and then safely tread
In this loves hallow'd temple, this soft bed.
In such white robes, heaven's Angels us'd to be
Receavd by men; Thou Angel bringst with thee
A heaven like Mahomets Paradise; and though
Ill spirits walk in white, we easly know,
By this these Angels from an evil sprite,
Those set our hairs, but these our flesh upright.
    Licence my roaving hands, and let them go,
Before, behind, between, above, below.
O my America! my new-found-land,
My kingdome, safeliest when with one man man'd,
My Myne of precious stones, My Emperie,
How blest am I in this discovering thee!
To enter in these bonds, is to be frees
Then where my hand is set, my seal shall be.

Full nakedness! All joyes are due to thee,
As souls unbodied, bodies uncloth'd must be,
To taste whole joyes. Gems which you women use
Are like Atlanta's balls, cast in mens views,
That when a fools eye lighteth on a Gem,
His earthly soul may covet theirs, not them.
Like pictures, or like books gay coverings made
For lay-men, are all women thus array'd;
Themselves are mystick books, which only wee
(Whom their imputed grace will dignifie)
Must see reveal'd. Then since that I may know;
As liberally, as to a Midwife, shew
Thy self: cast all, yea, this white lynnen hence,
There is no pennance due to innocence.
    To teach thee, I am naked first; why than
What needst thou have more covering then a man.

The Triple Foole

I am two fooles, I know,
For loving, and for saying so
    In whining Poëtry;
But where's that wiseman, that would not be I,
    If she would not deny?
Then as th'earths inward narrow crooked lanes
Do purge sea waters fretfull salt away,
    I thought, if I could draw my paines,
Through Rimes vexation, I should them allay,
Griefe brought to numbers cannot be so fierce,
For, he tames it, that fetters it in verse.

But when I have done so,
Some man, his art and voice to show,
    Doth Set and sing my paine,
And, by delighting many, frees againe
    Griefe, which verse did restraine.
To Love, and Griefe tribute of Verse belongs,
But not of such as pleases when'tis read,
    Both are increased by such songs:
For both their triumphs so are published,
And I, which was two fooles, do so grow three;
Who are a little wise, the best fooles bee.

Twicknam Garden

Blasted with sighs, and surrounded with teares,
    Hither I come to seeke the spring,
    And at mine eyes, and at mine eares,
Receive such balmes, as else cure every thing;
    But O, selfe traytor, I do bring
The spider love, which transubstantiates all,
    And can convert Manna to gall,
And that this place may thoroughly be thought
    True Paradise, I have the serpent brought.

'Twere wholsomer for mee, that winter did
    Benight the glory of this place,
    And that a grave frost did forbid
These trees to laugh, and mocke mee to my face;
    But that I may not this disgrace
Indure, nor yet leave loving, Love let mee
    Some senslesse peece of this place bee;
Make me a mandrake, so I may groane here,
    Or a stone fountaine weeping out my yeare.

Hither with christall vyals, lovers come,
    And take my teares, which are loves wine,
    And try your mistresse Teares at home,
For all are false, that tast not just like mine;
    Alas, hearts do not in eyes shine,
Nor can you more judge womans thoughts by teares,
    Then by her shadow, what she weares.
O perverse sexe, where none is true but shee,
    Who's therefore true, because her truth kills mee.

The Undertaking

I have done one braver thing
    Then all the *Worthies* did,
And yet a braver thence doth spring,
    Which is, to keepe that hid.

It were but madnes now t'impart
    The skill of specular stone,
When he which can have learn'd the art
    To cut it, can finde none.

So, if I now should utter this,
    Others (because no more
Such stuffe to worke upon, there is,)
    Would love but as before.

But he who lovelinesse within
    Hath found, all outward loathes,
For he who colour loves, and skinne,
    Loves but their oldest clothes.

If, as I have, you also doe
    Vertue'attir'd in woman see,
And dare love that, and say so too,
    And forget the Hee and Shee;

And if this love, though placed so,
    From prophane men you hide,
Which will no faith on this bestow,
    Or, if they doe, deride:

Then you have done a braver thing
    Then all the *Worthies* did;
And a braver thence will spring,
    Which is, to keepe that hid.

A Valediction: forbidding mourning

As virtuous men passe mildly away,
    And whisper to their soules, to goe,
Whilst some of their sad friends doe say,
    The breath goes now, and some say, no:

So let us melt, and make no noise,
    No teare-floods, nor sigh-tempests move,
T'were prophanation of our joyes
    To tell the layetie our love.

Moving of th'earth brings harmes and feares,
    Men reckon what it did and meant,
But trepidation of the spheares,
    Though greater farre, is innocent.

Dull sublunary lovers love
    (Whose soule is sense) cannot admit
Absence, because it doth remove
    Those things which elemented it.

But we by a love, so much refin'd,
    That our selves know not what it is,
Inter-assured of the mind,
    Care lesse, eyes, lips, and hands to misse.

Our two soules therefore, which are one,
    Though I must goe, endure not yet
A breach, but an expansion,
    Like gold to ayery thinnesse beate.

If they be two, they are two so
    As stiffe twin compasses are two,
Thy soule the fixt foot, makes no show
    To move, but doth, if the'other doe.

And though it in the center sit,
    Yet when the other far doth rome,
It leanes, and hearkens after it,
    And growes erect, as that comes home.

Such wilt thou be to mee, who must
    Like th'other foot, obliquely runne;
Thy firmnes makes my circle just,
    And makes me end, where I begunne.

A Valediction: of my name, in the window

I

    My name engrav'd herein,
Doth contribute my firmnanesse to this glasse,
  Which, ever since that charme, hath beene
  As hard, as that which grav'd it, was;
Thine eye will give it price enough, to mock
    The diamonds of either rock.

II

    'Tis much that Glasse should bee
As all confessing, and through-shine as I,
  'Tis more, that it shewes thee to thee,
  And cleare reflects thee to thine eye.
But all such rules, loves magique can undoe,
    Here you see mee, and I am you.

III

    As no one point, nor dash,
Which are but accessaries to this name,
  The showers and tempests can outwash,
  So shall all times finde mee the same;
You this intirenesse better may fulfill,
    Who have the patterne with you still.

IV

    Or if too hard and deepe
This learning be, for a scratch'd name to teach,
  It, as a given deaths head keepe,
  Lovers mortalitie to preach,
Or thinke this ragged bony name to bee
    My ruinous Anatomie.

V

    Then, as all my soules bee,
Emparadis'd in you, (in whom alone
  I understand, and grow and see,)
  The rafters of my body, bone
Being still with you, the Muscle, Sinew, and Veine,
    Which tile this house, will come againe:

VI

    Till my returne, repaire
And recompact my scattered body so.
  As all the vertuous powers which are
  Fix'd in the starres, are said to flow
Into such characters, as graved bee
    When these starres have supremacie:

VII

    So since this name was cut
When love and griefe their exaltation had,
  No doore 'gainst this names influence shut;
  As much more loving, as more sad,
'Twill make thee; and thou shouldst, till I returne,
    Since I die daily, daily mourne.

VIII

    When thy inconsiderate hand
Flings ope this casement, with my trembling name,
  To looke on one, whose wit or land,
  New battry to thy heart may frame,
Then thinke this name alive, and that thou thus
    In it offendst my Genius.

IX

    And when thy melted maid,
Corrupted by thy Lover's gold, and page,
   His letter at thy pillow'hath laid,
   Disputed it, and tam'd thy rage,
And thou begin'st to thaw towards him, for this,
      May my name step in, and hide his.

X

    And if this treason goe
To an overt act, and that thou write againe;
   In superscribing, this name flow
   Into thy fancy, from the pane.
So, in forgetting thou remembrest right,
And unaware to mee shalt write.

XI

    But glasse, and lines must bee,
No meanes our firme substantiall love to keepe;
   Neere death inflicts this lethargie,
   And this I murmure in my sleepe;
Impute this idle talke, to that I goe,
      For dying men talke often so.

A Valediction: of the booke

I'll tell thee now (deare Love) what thou shalt doe
   To anger destiny, as she doth us,
   How I shall stay, though she Esloygne me thus,
And how posterity shall know it too;
     How thine may out-endure
     Sybills glory, and obscure
     Her who from Pindar could allure,
   And her, through whose helpe *Lucan* is not lame,
And her, 'whose booke (they say) *Homer* did finde, and name.

Study our manuscripts, those Myriades
   Of letters, which have past twixt thee and mee,
   Thence write our Annals, and in them will bee
To all whom loves subliming fire invades,
     Rule and example found;
     There, the faith of any ground
     No schismatique will dare to wound,
   That sees, how Love this grace to us affords,
To make, to keep, to use, to be these his Records.

This Booke, as long-liv'd as the elements,
   Or as the worlds forme, this all-graved tome
   In cypher writ, or new made Idiome,
Wee for loves clergie only'are instruments:
     When this booke is made thus,
     Should againe the ravenous
     Vandals and Goths inundate us,
   Learning were safe; in this our Universe
Schooles might learne Sciences, Spheares Musick, Angels Verse.

Here Loves Divines, (since all Divinity
   Is love or wonder) may finde all they seeke,
   Whether abstract spirituall love they like,
Their Soules exhal'd with what they do not see,

Or, loth so to amuze
Faiths infirmitie, they chuse
Something which they may see and use;
For, though minde be the heaven, where love doth sit,
Beauty a convenient type may be to figure it.

Here more then in their bookes may Lawyers finde,
Both by what titles Mistresses are ours,
And how prerogative these states devours,
Transferr'd from Love himselfe, to womankinde,
Who though from heart, and eyes,
They exact great subsidies,
Forsake him who on them relies,
And for the cause, honour, or conscience give,
Chimeraes, vaine as they, or their prerogative.

Here Statesmen, (or of them, they which can reade,)
May of their occupation finde the grounds:
Love and their art alike it deadly wounds,
If to consider what 'tis, one proceed,
In both they doe excell
Who the present governe well,
Whose weaknesse none doth, or dares tell;
In this thy booke, such will their nothing see,
As in the Bible some can finde out Alchimy.

Thus vent thy thoughts; abroad I'll studie thee,
As he removes farre off, that great heights takes;
How great love is, presence best tryall makes,
But absence tryes how long this love will bee;
To take a latitude
Sun, or starres, are fitliest view'd
At their brightest, but to conclude
Of longitudes, what other way have wee,
But to marke when, and where the darke eclipses bee?

A Valediction: of weeping

      Let me powre forth
My teares before thy face, whil'st I stay here,
For thy face coines them, and thy stampe they beare,
And by this Mintage they are something worth,
      For thus they bee
      Pregnant of thee;
Fruits of much griefe they are, emblemes of more,
When a teare falls, that thou falst which it bore,
So thou and I are nothing then, when on a divers shore.

      On a round ball
A workeman that hath copies by, can lay
An Europe, Afrique, and an Asia,
And quickly make that, which was nothing, *All*,
      So doth each teare,
      Which thee doth weare,
A globe, yea world by that impression grow,
Till thy teares mixt with mine doe overflow
This world, by waters sent from thee, my heaven dissolved so.

      O more then Moone,
Draw not up seas to drowne me in thy spheare,
Weepe me not dead, in thine armes, but forbeare
To teach the sea, what it may doe too soone;
      Let not the winde
      Example finde,
To doe me more harme, then it purposeth;
Since thou and I sigh one anothers breath,
Who e'r sighes most, is cruellest, and hasts the others death.

The Will

Before I sigh my last gaspe, let me breath,
Great love, some Legacies; Here I bequeath
Mine eyes to *Argus,* if mine eyes can see,
If they be blinde, then Love, I give them thee;
My tongue to Fame; to'Embassadours mine eares;
    To women or the sea, my teares.
Thou, Love, hast taught mee heretofore
  By making mee serve her who'had twenty more,
That I should give to none, but such, as had too much before.

My constancie I to the planets give;
My truth to them, who at the Court doe live;
Mine ingenuity and opennesse,
To Jesuites; to Buffones my pensivenesse;
My silence to'any, who abroad hath beene;
    My mony to a Capuchin.
Thou Love taught'st me, by appointing mee
  To love there, where no love receiv'd can be,
Onely to give to such as have an incapacitie.

My faith I give to Roman Catholiques;
All my good works unto the Schismaticks
Of Amsterdam; my best civility
And Courtship, to an Universitie;
My modesty I give to souldiers bare;
    My patience let gamesters share.
Thou Love taughtst mee, by making mee
  Love her that holds my love disparity,
Onely to give to those that count my gifts indignity.

I give my reputation to those
Which were my friends; Mine industrie to foes;
To Schoolemen I bequeath my doubtfulnesse;
My sicknesse to Physitians, or excesse;
To Nature, all that I in Ryme have writ;
    And to my company my wit.
Thou Love, by making mee adore
Her, who begot this love in mee before,
Taughtst me to make, as though I gave, when I did but restore.

To him for whom the passing bell next tolls,
I give my physick bookes; my writen rowles
Of Morall counsels, I to Bedlam give;
My brazen medals, unto them which live
In want of bread; To them which passe among
    All forrainers, mine English tongue.
Thou, Love, by making mee love one
Who thinkes her friendship a fit portion
For yonger lovers, dost my gifts thus disproportion.

Therefore I'll give no more; But I'll undoe
The world by dying; because love dies too.
Then all your beauties will bee no more worth
Then gold in Mines, where none doth draw it forth;
And all your graces no more use shall have
    Then a Sun dyall in a grave.
Thou Love taughtst mee, by making mee
Love her, who doth neglect both mee and thee,
To'invent, and practise this one way, to'annihilate all three.

Witchcraft by a picture

I fixe mine eye on thine, and there
   Pitty my picture burning in thine eye,
My picture drown'd in a transparent teare,
    When I looke lower I espie;
      Hadst thou the wicked skill
By pictures made and mard, to kill,
How many wayes mightst thou performe thy will?

But now I have drunke thy sweet salt teares,
   And though thou poure more I'll depart;
My picture vanish'd, vanish feares;
    That I can be endamag'd by that art;
      Though thou retaine of mee
One picture more, yet that will bee,
Being in thine owne heart, from all malice free.

Womans Constancy

Now thou hast lov'd me one whole day,
To morrow when thou leav'st, what wilt thou say?
Wilt thou then Antedate some new made vow?
     Or say that now
We are not just those persons, which we were?
Or, that oathes made in reverentiall feare
Of Love, and his wrath, any may forsweare?
Or, as true deaths, true maryages untie,
So lovers contracts, images of those,
Binde but till sleep, deaths image, them unloose?
     Or, your owne end to Justifie,
For having purpos'd change, and falsehood; you
Can have no way but falsehood to be true?
Vaine lunatique, against these scapes I could
     Dispute, and conquer, if I would,
      Which I abstaine to doe,
For by to morrow, I may thinke so too.